The Island Queen

Jean Bovell

JEAN BOVELL

November 2015

Published by Dolman Scott Ltd
Copyright Jean Bovell 2015

ISBN: 978-1-909204-69-0

Dolman Scott Ltd
www.dolmanscott.co.uk

Introduction

*T*he *Island Queen* is the true story of an unprecedented excursion of pleasure that captured the imagination of an island nation.

The year was 1944 and the majority on the small island of Grenada knew of the advertised journey of partying on the schooner *Island Queen* scheduled for the forthcoming August Bank Holiday weekend. The people were fascinated. It was the first time that such an event had occurred on the island.

In particular, the atmosphere around the island's city of St George buzzed in anticipation of what was purported to be "the most exciting activity of 1944". St George's had been the home town of the well-known owner of the schooner *Island Queen* and also the vast majority of "would-be" participants on the fun-packed overnight voyage to the island of St Vincent.

The story of *The Island Queen* is very much centred on the era. It tells of how people lived during World War 2 on the "sister" islands encountered by the party vessel as she headed towards her destination. Life as it used to be in the homeland of Grenada, the home-town of St George and the effects of war are also incorporated within the narrative.

The various social activities that occurred during the unforgettable August Bank Holiday weekend of 1944 are featured, but with significant focus on the much-anticipated journey of pleasure that began with high-spirited jubilation and wonderful expectations.

The Island Queen is an interesting and at times moving story. It touches on different life experiences, themes and human emotions.

Jean Bovell

Acknowledgements

This book is dedicated to Lloyd, Augustine Radix.

It was because of Lloyd's suggestion that this project was initiated.

Thank you,

Edward David, Peter Francis, Miriam Francis, Martin George, Wilbert Harris, Evelyn Henry, Thomas Henry, Phylis Hypolite, Dr Joan Plange, Maria Quarless, Dr Michael Radix, Dr Roger Radix, Robert Rowley, Pamela Steele and Beryl Stanislaus.

The story was enhanced by the factual information you provided. Your personal disclosures lent insight and emotional depth to the narrative.

Thank you, Mary Curran for your interest and practical support.

Grenada and St Vincent national newspapers of the period accessed from: The British Library, London, England.

Factual documentations relating to the schooner Island Queen were made available by The National Archives, London, England.

Contents:

Setting Sale 1

The Sister Isles 11

Homeland...15

Home Town 21

Impact of War..37

Saturday 5th August 1944 47

The Excursion Schooners......................................49

The Excursion is underway – 5th August 1944 53

How They Partied at Home 61

A Journey of Pleasure 67

The Island of St Vincent...71

Crucial Days 73

The Mood of the People...91

Search and Surveillance 101

Reaction in St Vincent 105

The Search is Called Off.......................................109

Reaction to News Most Feared 115

Lost Souls...123

Personal Accounts of How the Tragedy Impacted............127

They Stepped Back from the Brink 133

Action Taken by the Government of Grenada 137

The Aftermath of the Official Enquiry 153

The end of World War 2 157

Time Heals...161

Hypotheses...165

A Mystery of the Sea 169

The Island Queen

The true story of an unprecedented journey of pleasure in Caribbean waters during World War 2.

Setting Sail

The world was at war. And from around February 1942 allied shipments of essential minerals such as oil, aluminium and molasses from the Caribbean to North America and Europe were being intercepted, torpedoed and sunk by German warships and submarines. Warfare raged in Caribbean waters until 1944, when German ships withdrew from the area after coming under heavy and extensive bombardment from Allied Naval Forces that had been expanded and reinforced.

During the period in the Caribbean when Allied and German ships were being slammed into, attacked and sunk, the people who lived on the Caribbean islands, to a greater or lesser degree, experienced shortages in essential commodities and merchandise. But, despite ongoing sea battles, trading of goods between the various islands which were usually conveyed by boat, continued.

On the island of Grenada, a regular boat service had been in operation. Locally built and privately owned vessels transported not just much-required essentials but also people to and from other islands in the region. Among these vessels was a particular schooner called *Island Queen*. And it was on the schooner *Island Queen* that a pleasure excursion from Grenada to St Vincent had been organised. The trip was planned to occur over the August Bank Holiday weekend. The schooner *Island Queen* was scheduled to depart from St George's harbour, Grenada, on Saturday, 5th August 1944 and return on Wednesday, 9th August 1944.

FLASH ! FLASH !!

Excursion to St. Vincent
By Auxiliary Schooner
"ISLAND QUEEN"

Contact :

GORDON A. CAMPBELL,
at 4 Halifax Street, St. George's,
ô or before Saturday July 29th, 1944,

Advertisement for the Excursion to St. Vincent in *The West Indian* Newspaper

The definitive advertisement

The August Bank Holiday weekend was one of several annual national holidays celebrated, even in war time, on the island of Grenada. And when the advertisement of the planned pleasure excursion appeared in the island's main newspaper, *The West Indian*, it caught the eye of many young Grenadians of the day. The privileged young people who resided in the Island's city, St George's, were particularly interested. These city-dwellers moved in the same social circle as the Captain of the schooner *Island Queen* and his family and knew him well. They were instinctively aware that the excursion had been targeted essentially towards people of "their kind", and were, as a consequence, excited about the prospect of partying all the way to St Vincent in company with close friends and relatives. But the nation as a whole was enthralled. The *Island Queen* pleasure excursion had been "a first" as far as Grenadians were concerned, and news of the event was passed on by word of mouth across the land.

Just six weeks after the party trip was advertised, 5th August 1944 arrived and the Bank Holiday weekend was upon the nation. An air of optimism and joyful expectation swept throughout the land and every man, woman and child welcomed the break from school or work, and looked forward to being involved in some form of family, friendship or organised sporting or social activity. For the community in the city of St George, the departure of the much-anticipated "never before" party trip to St Vincent on the schooner *Island Queen* at the beginning of the holiday weekend provided additional buzz to the holiday spirit that existed within the town. And even though it was common knowledge that only the "better off" among them would be participating in the excursion, everyone who lived in the town of the period had been fascinated by what was considered an historical and never-to-be-forgotten social adventure.

The island's city of St George, a quaint little town defined by narrow roads and hilly terrain, lay on the southern coastline. One of the main institutions in the town had been the Catholic Cathedral, which stood imposingly at the top of a central hill overlooking the hustle and bustle of everyday life beneath. The Cathedral was symbolised by a large-faced clock and its chimes, which regularly and reliably at quarterly intervals tunefully chimed the time of day, were often accompanied by catchy lyrics. Indeed, the chorus: "I don't tell lies, Scot's Church tells lies. I don't tell lies..." were often chanted in rhythmic tones to the background of chiming church bells by a number of young children who lived in the town of the day.

The harbour, St George's Grenada.

And so it was, in a fleeting but most memorable moment in time on the evening of 5th August 1944, four hours after the scheduled time of departure, the schooner *Island Queen* slowly manoeuvred its way out of the town's harbour as six intermittent gongs from the landmark clock thundered throughout the tiny town.

The passengers stood on the deck of the schooner and waved furiously and ecstatically in response to loud cheers from relatives, friends and well-wishers standing at the water front. The happy revellers included some of the most beautiful and fashionable young women who lived in the town of St George during the period. These striking-looking individuals were attractively attired in colourful dresses or full or pleated knee-length skirts, into which co-ordinating blouses had been tucked, and with broad-brimmed straw hats secured firmly on their heads and carrying patterned straw bags they stood on the deck of the schooner *Island Queen*, alongside good-looking young men sporting blazers over open-necked shirts and donning colourful hats. Several teenage school-girls in pretty dresses and panama school hats were also among the group. The picture-perfect scene depicting the beaming faces of privileged young people, joyfully embarking on the highly anticipated celebratory excursion to St Vincent on that clear, bright and sunny day in August 1944 would be etched in the memory of every relative, friend, well-wisher and bystander who witnessed the extraordinary moment.

Approximately thirty minutes after the departure of the schooner *Island Queen*, a smaller schooner, the *Providence Mark*, left the harbour on a parallel journey to St Vincent.

The schooner *Providence Mark* had been commissioned because of the unexpected and overwhelming demand for tickets by individuals keen to participate in the advertised pleasure excursion on the schooner *Island Queen*. It became apparent that two and not just one vessel would be necessary for a journey that appeared to have caught the imagination of so many, and the decision was taken to hire a second vessel for carrying the people who applied for tickets after all places on the schooner *Island Queen* had been taken. As a consequence, the schooner *Providence Mark* had not been the primary choice for those who had set their hearts on partying all the way to St Vincent. But many who preferred a quieter or more restful voyage were content to be travelling on the second schooner, whose "send off" had been, in comparison to that of the schooner *Island Queen*, very much low key. But the noisy fanfaronade that accompanied the previous departure may have been in part a reflection of the collective feeling of happy relief that, after a delay of four hours, the "good time" vessel was finally on her way.

Indeed, the privileged individuals who had secured tickets for travelling on the preferred vessel felt "lucky" and could hardly wait for the "rave" to begin. But the mood had been soured four hours prior to the actual departure. The schooner *Island Queen* was scheduled to leave St George's harbour bound for St Vincent at around 2.00 pm on Saturday, 5th August 1944, but a significant number of individuals with tickets to travel on the schooner *Providence Mark* defiantly boarded the primary pleasure schooner and stubbornly refused to budge. Mayhem descended as tempers flared; but when the melee was at fever-pitch and appeared intransigent, a decision was taken to moor both vessels to a different position on the pier, where a calm process of negotiation and compromise was initiated.

Any suggestion of setting sail an overloaded vessel was non-negotiable as far as the Captain of the *Island Queen* was concerned, and this stance may have been based primarily on issues relating to the health and safety of his passengers. These firmly held principles no doubt influenced the Captain's decision that all minors should travel on the schooner *Island Queen*, thus ensuring his exclusive supervision and safeguard of the children's well-being.

As the deliberations proceeded, many individuals who had initially considered themselves fortunate to have "bagged" tickets for the schooner *Island Queen* agreed to swap with specific individuals that had been assigned to the *Providence Mark*, many of whom wished to be with sweethearts, siblings or close friends on the schooner *Island Queen*. But these compromisers were in the main "fed up" with the long delay and were anxious to get going. The protests eventually came to an end when the majority expressed satisfaction with their separate negotiated trading of tickets. And the passengers were thrilled when, after what appeared to be an eternity, the imminent departure of the pleasure schooner *Island Queen* was at long last announced by her Captain.

The schooner *Island Queen*, with its cargo of not just luggage but also musicians, handsome young men and beautiful girls, had undoubtedly been a seductive prospect to those who were intent on not missing out on what was expected to be a highly enjoyable and memorable journey. A retired engineer who was just a boy at the time of the *Island Queen* excursion recalled his father, a devoted family man and respected Civil Servant, actually borrowing the money required for buying a ticket for the excursion from his own mother and paternal grandmother of the young lad. The young husband and father had been forbidden by his wife from funding the trip from the family budget. Not only did she feel that, with a family to support, their money could be put to better use, the young wife and mother had an uncanny feeling or premonition that her husband should not participate in the pleasure excursion. But the husband was not deterred and remained determined. Looking back, our informant believes that his father may have desired a brief respite of youthful fun. And having the chance to party in company with beautiful girls on the schooner *Island Queen*, all the way to St Vincent, may have been too much of a "pull" to resist.

The majority of young holiday-makers on the party schooner had been the "cream" of the then city society. They were members of an exclusive club consisting of an attractive, self-confident and vivacious group of "entitled" boys and girls. Many had been life-long neighbourhood friends or were related to or on friendly terms with the Captain of the schooner *Island Queen*. Indeed, applications to join the excursion from individuals known to be within the Captain's social circle had been given priority of place. These persons included professional practitioners, civil servants, teachers and business entrepreneurs. And several had recently completed higher education and were on the cusp of rewarding careers. The party participants on the schooner *Island Queen* had been, without doubt, kindred spirits and the majority "hung" together. The minors, aged between thirteen and sixteen, were the offspring of comparatively wealthy parents and attended fee-paying secondary schools on the island.

And so it was, after a considerable period of presented challenges, heated arguments and intransigence, a compromise solution was reached and the schooner *Island Queen* was eventually on her way. And as she sailed, sounds of jovial singing and chattering mingled with shrieks of laughter and music playing in the background left little doubt in the minds of those left behind that very little time had been wasted in starting the party. But the noises from the vessel, which were clearly heard by individuals who lived or lingered along the island's coastlines or hilltops overlooking the sea, faded as the schooner steered further and further into open waters. Issues relating to safety or risks may not have even entered the minds of the young high-spirited and advantaged passengers as they engaged in merry-making on the holiday schooner. They may have simply taken for granted the fact that the Skipper at the helm had been well known and respected for being a skilled, competent and experienced seaman. There were, as a consequence, "no worries".

As the schooner *Island Queen* headed northward on the 136.98-mile fun-filled voyage to St Vincent, she would have sailed past the sister isles of Carriacou and Petite Martinique. These islands, although being among the Grenadines, a string of islands leading on to St Vincent, are nonetheless part of the three-island state of Grenada. The remaining Grenadine islands are within the territory known as St Vincent and the Grenadines.

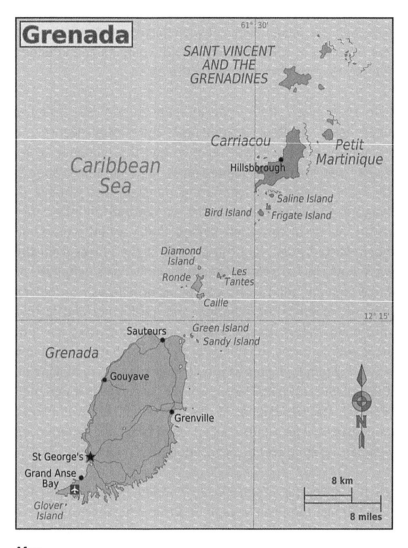

Map

The Sister Isles

G renada had been the homeland of the vast majority of the young people who boarded the schooner *Island Queen* for the much-anticipated journey of partying all the way to St Vincent, on that fateful day in August 1944.

Grenada is the largest of three small islands which include Carriacou and Petite Martinique. The tri-island state, commonly known as the "sister-isles", is unified under one governing body and judiciary; and educational, employment and business systems are all inclusive. The islands share a national flag and can be collectively called Grenada. The *Island Queen* excursion occurred during a period when boats were used for the daily commute between the islands. Many individuals who lived in Carriacou and Petite Martinique attended school, worked, went on shopping trips or visited friends and relatives who lived on mainland Grenada.

Despite the fundamental shared culture that prevailed, the sub-culture and way of life on the separate islands were identifiably unique.

The island of Carriacou lies north of Grenada. It measures 13 square miles (34 kilometres) and is the largest of the chain of islands known as the Grenadines. The Grenadines are situated between the islands of Grenada and St Vincent.

The scenic "sister-isle" of Carriacou, with her magnificent views of the ocean and neighbouring islands, and wide stretches of untouched silver-sand beaches, would have been the first island encountered by the schooner *Island Queen* during her voyage to St Vincent. Carriacou's main industries during the period of the *Island Queen* excursion were fishing, cotton, peanuts and livestock. Various species of farm animals naturally inhabited the island; and there had been regular transporting by boat from Carriacou to mainland Grenada of peanuts, cotton and livestock, such as goats, lambs, pigs and cattle.

Many boats used for the lucrative trading of goods between Carriacou and Grenada and vice versa had been built locally. The Carriacou community was at the time commonly known as "boat builders" or "boat people". And while Grenadian young men of the period also built and owned their own boats, Grenville being the well-known town for boat-building, the majority strived towards owning a bicycle, motor-bike or even a car; their contemporaries on the island of Carriacou actively pursued a keen interest in building and owning their own boat. Many read literature on the subject and there were those who enrolled in Marine schools in foreign countries before embarking as qualified seamen on successful maritime careers. Indeed, husbands and fathers of better-off Carriacouan families of the era captained ships world-wide and were absent from home for long periods, returning to their families just once or maybe twice in any one year.

The population of Carriacou, which had been approximately 4,000 at the time of the *Island Queen* excursion, shared a communal and strong sense of identity and belonging, but were known to be friendly and welcoming to foreign visitors. The people enjoyed a unique sub-cultural way of life. Their boat-building and sailing skills were demonstrated at the annual "Regatta", a racing event for locally built boats. The island's proud tradition in music and dance was reflected during the "Perang" festival, which is celebrated during the weekend prior to Christmas. And the "Big Drum" festival was a spirited and captivating exhibition of ritual dance performed around beating drums by dancers dressed in tribal costume. The cultural event, rooted in African ancestry, would have been one of a variety of social activities enjoyed by the people of Carriacou during the holiday weekend of 5th August 1944.

The revellers on the schooner *Island Queen* would also have experienced a splendid view of Petite Martinique on their journey to St Vincent. Petite Martinique is a land mass consisting of 586 acres (34 kilometres). It is the smallest island within the three-island state of Grenada.

Petite Martinique was an exquisite and undisturbed miniature land land which produced cotton and peanuts. The community was small and familiar. Family homes and amenities such as shops, church and school were all within short walking distances. The sub-culture of Petite Martinique to a large degree had been very similar to that of Carriacou. In particular, many people who lived on the island of Petite Martinique were, at the time of the *Island Queen* excursion, boat-builders and boat owners. But there were also the academically ambitious who achieved successful professional careers not only in Grenada but also in foreign countries such as the United States of America.

There were elementary schools in both Carriacou and Petite Martinique, but children from relatively well-off families or those on scholarships attended Secondary schools on mainland Grenada. Children from the sister islands who received secondary education on the mainland often boarded with family friends or relatives during term-time. It had also been a time when various individuals from Carriacou and Petite Martinique lived and worked on the island of Grenada.

Similar to the people of Grenada and Carriacou, folk on the tiny island of Petite Martinique would have had the option of engaging in a variety of functions during the 1944 August Bank Holiday weekend. These may have included family gatherings, organised sporting events or social dances.

But there could be no other option for the passengers on board the schooner *Island Queen* as she cruised past the various islands on her night-long journey of pleasure to the island of St Vincent.

Homeland

As their journey began, the vast number of pleasure-seekers on board the schooner *Island Queen* waved cheerfully to family, friends and well-wishers who had come to the pier to see them off. But the vast majority were also bidding farewell to mainland Grenada, the beloved land of their birth.

The island of Grenada is a hilly and mountainous mass with fertile plantations and just 133 square miles in circumference. The population at the time of the *Island Queen* excursion had been approximately 95,000, comprising peoples of European, East Indian and African descent. The majority (80%) of Grenadians were of African descent.

Large numbers of the population lived in "the country", the common term used for parishes outside of the island's capital, St. George's. There was a separate town in each parish. These towns were situated in close proximity to the coast and each town contained a minimum of one local government building, a post office, police station and at least one Christian church and elementary Christian school. Various places of business in these towns included retail outlets and open markets.

The majority of children in country areas attended their local elementary school, while relatively few received access to secondary education. During the period that the schooner *Island Queen* embarked on her journey of pleasure to St Vincent, the island's secondary schools were located in the city of St George. These prestigious schools were fee-paying and affordable only by comparatively well-off families. But a scholarship was awarded on an annual basis by each secondary school and academically bright children up and down the island competed against each other for the coveted solitary scholarship.

For the most part, children in country areas endured a "hard" life consisting of various routine chores, which included looking after livestock and working the land. These children received very little appreciation for their efforts. Parental nurturing was rare and toys displayed in shop windows during the Christmas season were usually found in the Christmas stockings that were hung by children who were from comparatively well-off families. This fact may have stirred the imagination of ordinary children in country areas, as the natural resources by which they were surrounded were used, particularly by young boys of the day, for designing and constructing a variety of play devices. These included cricket bats carved from the branches of coco-nut trees and small but firm oranges being used as balls for playing the much-loved and competitive game of cricket. Bamboo strips became frames on which paper was constructed into kites and flown in contest fashion during the Easter period. Wood cut from trees was shaved and sculpted into spinning wooden tops. The tops of "throw-away" cans were dislodged and used for engaging in "sword-like" games. Discarded bicycle wheels became vehicles that were balanced and steered by sticks. All the while, fishing, swimming, diving and hunting for wild game continued to be a historical pastime enjoyed by country children all over the island of Grenada.

Even though children raised in country areas of the time were comparatively deprived and subjected to regimes of labour and very little appreciation, every moment of leisure had been fully appreciated. These youngsters may have worked hard, but when given the opportunity, they played hard.

Telling "Nancy stories" to children before retiring to bed at night had been a common occurrence in homes throughout the land. "Nancy stories", usually recounted by an elder in the family, were scary, ghostly yarns that had been passed down the generational line. These spooky and ghostly tales were designed to send shivers down the spines of young listeners and never failed to result in restless nights and sleep that was interrupted by alarming and terrifying nightmares.

The range of adult occupations within country communities of the day ensured the interdependent link necessary for the smooth functioning of any society, and included labourers, domestics, fishermen, estate owners, farm workers, bakers and butchers. There was also a variety of skilled practitioners such as healthcare workers, civil servants, teachers and business entrepreneurs. Like most communities, comparative class divisions, based on occupation, land ownership or even the size of a person's dwelling, were in existence. Family homes in country areas of the period ranged from one-room wooden shacks to four- or five-room wall houses built on two floors, the upper floor being accessed by steps constructed on the exterior. But home for a large number of "country people" had been a humble two-room "board house". These were simple souls with few expectations who were content with their "lot" in life. They were sustained by their Christian Faith, and an enduring sense of family belonging and national patriotism that transcended material partitions.

There was, however, essentially, no real poverty, as hunger had been unheard of by people who lived in country areas of the day. The land yielded plenty of food and many families rented, purchased or inherited at least one plot of productive land. The wide variety of wholesome and healthy produce provided substantive nutrition. In particular, the breadfruit, a nutty and versatile vegetable which could be boiled, fried or roasted and served with or without accompaniment, had been widely popular. Breadfruit was also the main vegetable used for making the nation's favourite dish, "Oil Down". The communal generosity of spirit within country areas ensured a willingness to share with each other the natural produce reaped from separate plots of land. However, the custom did in no way deter unscrupulous individuals secretly helping themselves, from other people's property, to the plumpest fruit or fullest vegetables before land-owners were even aware that the planted crop was ready for picking!

Spices had been an exclusively valuable product yielded and evident by the intrinsic exquisite aroma of the countryside. In particular, the scents exuded from mace that had been laid out to dry on covered open ground was sweetly potent. Mace, the outer red-coloured skin of the nutmeg, can be used for medicinal purposes and is a lucrative component of the nutmeg. The nutmeg had been one of the island's main industries and a reliable source of income from which even small land-ownership families in country areas benefited.

It was a statutory requirement that nutmeg transactions were documented in a billing book validating identity and land ownership. The book was presented to a designated officer at the "nutmeg pool" prior to the initiation of any legitimate sale of nutmeg. A percentage of the selling price was withheld and, combined with any subsequent increase in buying prices, would be returned on a regular basis to individual nutmeg vendors. This was commonly known as "back pay" and was very much anticipated. "Back pay" was often used for purchasing items of furniture, funding trips abroad or banking. At the time of the *Island Queen* excursion, Grenada nutmeg had been the source of lucrative earnings. Following the bombing of Pearl Harbor in 1941, shipments of nutmeg from the Far East to Europe and America had been terminated. This resulted in Grenada nutmeg being in high demand and prices "hit the roof".

Fishing was also a profitable industry and particularly abundant in country towns such as Gouyave in the parish of St John's and Grenville in the parish of St Andrew's.

Despite the comparatively humble existence of country folk, they were no less integral to a patriotic "One nation, One family" compassionate island community with an overall shared culture. Similar to other Caribbean communities, Grenadians, in general, held unshakeable Christian beliefs alongside a vibrant celebratory cultural spirit. And the Bank Holiday weekend of 5th August 1944 had indeed been a time for celebration.

Home Town

S t George's, the island's city, had been the home town of
many of the youthful passengers on the schooner *Island
Queen*. Relatives, friends and well-wishes who witnessed the
ship's departure had been dazzled by the beauty and vibrancy
of the young female excursionists as the vessel exited the
dock to begin her journey of pleasure to St Vincent.

The St George's of the age was a cramped little city with
plenty of character. It consisted of rugged narrow streets
and steep hills dotted with potholes, plateaus and unevenly
paved stone steps that led to upper and lower levels. Rows
of private and public brick buildings stood side by side in
an unmethodical and casual environment, where business
workers, public service employees and town dwellers
worked, lived and played. Christian churches and schools
were well-known landmarks, but the market square

located in the centre of the town had been a significant benchmark.

At a time when supermarkets, frozen products and private ownership of refrigerators were rare or non-existent on the island, food products were freshly consumed and town dwellers depended on traders from "the country" for the daily provision of fresh eggs, milk, fish, meat, fruit and vegetables.

The market place had been a bustling "hub" of humanity and activity within the island's tiny city of St George's; and every morning market traders, usually women, from country areas could be seen piling out of crammed buses and being assisted with unloading from the rear section of the vehicle baskets packed with their wares. The women would proceed to carefully display their land-sourced products on grounds in the trading section of the market. These items were guaranteed to be snapped up by city-dwellers and included a variety of home-made sauces and jams, coconut oil, coconut candy, corn on the cob, cashew nuts, sugar cane, cocoa balls, various spices, tropical fruit and root vegetables.

Market vendors were not the only commuters. These privately owned buses also carried people from country areas who worked in the city and children who attended the town's secondary schools. And farm animals secured with ropes were transported at the back of the bus, an area designated mainly for baggage and such-like. In those days buses were brightly painted open vehicles. There was a single entry and exit point at the end of each bench-row of seats; and seat-rows were separated by wood panels or posts. In a period when there was just one return bus journey on week days to St George's from the various country areas, being left behind at the end of the working or school day was not an option. And it was not unusual to see men and boys, unable to find a space on crowded buses, clutching courageously onto wooden posts or panels while standing precariously on ledges outside of buses that steered shakily round sharp corners situated on the edge of steep precipices, or climbed precariously over mountainous terrain and skidded at speed down bumpy hills.

The destination of buses had been indicated by the distinctive name that was decoratively but boldly printed at the front and back of each bus. These named buses included "GAIETY", "WESTERN HOPE", "LITTLE SUNSHINE", "FLORIDA PRIDE", "GRAND CENTRAL" and "COMFORT". Everyone knew which named bus went where. There were no signed bus stops, but passengers were assured that they would be "let off" at any requested point along the route.

There were various restaurants, clubs and rum shops scattered round the town of the period. Rum shops were places visited essentially by men for the purpose of socialising with each other over a drink or participating in card games or dominoes. Social venues also included a designated covered area in the market place where savoury snacks such as patties, cool drinks, snow cones or ice cream could be purchased. With its parked buses, taxis, vendors with their open displays of products for sale and haggling purchasers, the market place had been a thoroughfare of noisy, bustling humanity and a popular meeting point for friends and associates.

The market had also been the venue for national events such as political rallies, annual public commemorative festivals and parades involving cadets, Girl Guides and Boy Scouts marching in time with the Police Band. These were hugely popular occasions, attended by large numbers of people. Presentations in the market square were usually received with enthusiasm, viewed with interest, heard with attentive ears and punctuated by passionate cheering or even boos and jeering. The audience never failed to engage in spontaneous thunderous responses at the end of every commemoration, meeting or demonstration held in the market square of the day.

The ordinary majority looked forward with expectation and anticipation to the celebrations which were held in "the market" every "old year's" night. A large number of people would congregate in the square and with bated breath wait excitedly for church bells to chime in the New Year. At that point the crowd would erupt in a chorus of ecstatic cheering and wild, indiscriminate, affectionate embraces, followed by the beating of steel drums and delirious dancing and singing. And an illuminating ray of hope of better days to come was generated by the "out with the old", "in with the new" cultural expressions.

The St George's arm of the Salvation Army, clad in distinctive uniform, gathered in the market place every Sunday. They would sing songs integral to their uniquely conducted homily to a background of hitting tambourines and beating bongos. Individuals of all ages within the community looked forward to participating in the joyously infectious ritual delivered by the Salvation Army. And after returning from separate Sunday services, which may have been Roman Catholic, Church of England or Methodist, people would join the Salvation Army assembly, and gustily belt out well-known popular choruses while heartily clapping hands and stomping feet in time to tuneful rhythms. It was indeed a religious experience that offered a profound "feel-good" factor that was both energising and exhilarating. Although Catholics of the period had been in the majority, people were generally tolerant of each other's choices with regard to religion. And a person's specific Christian Faith was never considered an issue.

"The market" was also the starting point for bands during the carnival celebrations held annually on the Monday and Tuesday before Ash Wednesday. Ash Wednesday is a date in the Christian calendar signifying the beginning of Lent, a six-week period of sacrifice prior to Easter. The various bands in their separate colourful costumes that reflected a particular theme or subject would file from "the market" – in dance fashion, accompanied by calypso-playing steel drums. The carnival procession would progress along the narrow roads of the city and were joined at various points by hip-rotating individuals that were hypnotically propelled by the exciting sounds of music. Many danced the "jump up", a free-style, energetic dance executed by jumping to the beat in abandoned fashion. The "road march" was the most popular and tunefully rhythmic calypso of the season. It was the song that had been voted winner of the calypso singer/songwriter competition that was held each year prior to carnival and the signature calypso played and belted out by "carnival players" during the festivities.

The highlight of the two-day pageant was held at Queen's Park, the town's main venue for competitive sporting events such as football and cricket. The carnival pageant orchestrated at Queen's Park included competitions between the different bands, calypso singers/composers and steel drum players. Each act would be judged not only by the designated panel of judges, but also by members of the large number of seated spectators who would protest noisily and forcefully if they disagreed with the judges' final decisions. But the event never failed to end on a happy note for the majority. Everyone looked forward to the finale, which took the form of a beauty competition. This involved the introduction of the best-looking girls on the island who chose to enter the competition and the line-up would trigger not only cheers but wolf-whistles, nudges, winks and hilarious suggestive comments peppered with laughter, from groups of local young men among the spectators. The beauty judged "the winner" was crowned "Carnival Queen" of the particular year. And the crowning would be received by a standing ovation intermingled with boos and jeers, depending on whether or not a person's favourite girl had been the chosen one.

The market was not the only centre of trade in the city of St George's. There were a variety of retail outlets in the town. These included bakeries, drug stores, and small hardware or grocery stores which provided mainly imported items such as toothpaste, soap, salt, corn flakes, cheese, powdered or tinned milk, biscuits, flour and rice. Items including different types of material such as cotton, linen or silk, footwear, jewellery, utensils, glassware, china, furniture, various gadgets and vehicle spare parts could be purchased from one or other of the various departmental stores, several Syrian-owned, that were located within the vicinity of the city.

Men and women's outfits of the era were largely self-made or produced by skilled seamstresses or tailors. The everyday mode of dress for the ordinary majority of the town's community reflected the casual ambience of the then society. Men wore string vests, commonly known as merinos, over khaki pants. Women with plaited hair were dressed in bodices tucked into colourful flared skirts with large pockets. Both men and women wore comfortable footwear such as sandals or plimsolls as they strolled effortlessly along uncluttered streets.

Garments received by individuals from relatives or friends who lived in the United States were considered most fashionable. It was a period when America's doors had been open to the people of the Caribbean and those who were there for work or study reported "rich pickings". It had been the age of Swing Music and popular American songs such as "Boogie Woogie Bugle Boy", "Shoo Shoo Baby" and "I'll be Home for Christmas" were being transmitted on the radio. There were also the famous "film stars" that were featured in exciting movies such as "Tennessee Johnson", "There is Magic in the Music", "Moon over her Shoulder" and "Castle on the Hudson". It was altogether a combination of factors that lifted spirits and contributed towards the glamorisation of America and all things American by a large number of young Grenadians of the generation.

There was one British-owned bank whose employees were generally of British descent. But the "Penny Bank" was also in existence and provided a service to less well-off members of the community and also children.

The Carenage, an area bordering the sea-front on which the town's harbour is located, had been the "core" of the island's business community. The Carenage was also the stretch of road on which lay the island's main Post Office, Customs Office, Fire Station, Government Offices and cinema.

The General Hospital stood on high ground overlooking the Carenage. But healthcare at the time had not been easily accessible and many people in the town visited drug stores for purchasing tried and tested remedies such as Bay Rum for relieving head pain, Castor Oil for settling stomach upsets and Smelling Salts were used for overcoming conditions such as fainting episodes caused by the heat, dizzy spells or general feelings of disorientation. Vaccinations were not available and many children endured childhood illnesses such as measles, whooping cough or even polio. The most dreaded condition in adults was tuberculosis, a disease of the lung commonly known as TB. It was not only contagious and debilitating, but was also in those days a hugely feared incurable disease.

Policemen in crisp white-shirted uniforms and regimental caps regularly patrolled the streets of the town. In those days crime committed on persons or property had been few and far between occurrences. This "taken for granted" reality had no doubt been a contributory factor to the relaxed and trustful lifestyle of the era that included front doors being left unlocked and open and welcoming to all visitors during day time. On the rare occasion of a murder being committed, the sensational news would reverberate throughout the land and explode into a national tirade of shock and horror responses. It seemed unbelievable to the largely law-abiding and God-fearing nation that anyone was actually capable of perpetrating such an evil deed. It had been a time when the death sentence was not discretionary and was mandatory by law. And any man or woman found guilty of murder was promptly hanged. The old folk say that "the market" in St George's town was, at one stage in the island's history, a place for public execution!

There was indeed a comparatively vibrant and progressive community in the town of St George's at the time of the *Island Queen*'s pleasure excursion to St Vincent in August 1944. Many families lived in apartments above shops and stores or in houses within central areas of the town. Each house or apartment was electrically wired and equipped with running water, shower and flushing toilet. When the *Island Queen* sailed, radio, which transmitted news from the overseas British Broadcasting Corporation and music and songs from America, had already been introduced to the island. Telephones were also accessible, but these technologies were owned mainly by the relatively wealthy within the community.

Among those who witnessed the departure of the schooner *Island Queen* were the people who lived in The Bungalows. The Bungalows, situated in close proximity to the town's harbour, had been a government housing project which provided rented self-contained accommodation to less advantaged families in the community. It was a scheme that offered the opportunity for poor renters to eventually own and occupy a place of their own. People on the project who reliably and consistently paid their rent on or before the required time, for a stipulated period, were rewarded by being granted free ownership of their particular unit. Bungalow dwellers were a close and supportive sub-community within the town. A woman who was raised in The Bungalows told of her memories of being a member of a poor but happy brotherhood of people where everyone helped and supported each other. An example was that her grandmother owned the only oven in the neighbourhood. It was an outdoor stone-built oven and every family who lived on the project used it for baking their bread, cakes and ham at Christmas time. And there was communal sharing of all cooked or baked food on Christmas Day. The Christmas season had been special and a particular time of sharing and togetherness for The Bungalow dwellers.

Education of children had been a national priority. There were elementary Faith schools throughout the island. In those days religious studies had been integral to a curriculum that echoed subjects taught in British schools. Despite its definition, elementary schools provided a comprehensive education. Students were required to attend school on a regular basis until the age of 16, at which point school-leaving examinations would be set. On the last day of term, each school leaver was handed a certificate detailing his or her overall progress and academic achievements.

The island's secondary schools were also Faith-based but single-sexed, and all secondary schools of the day were located in St George's town. English Language, English Literature, English History and Maths were among the compulsory subjects delivered. Secondary schools were accessible to children from all backgrounds, as long as families were able to afford the required fee at the beginning of each term. But each secondary school offered one scholarship on an annual basis. And exceptionally bright elementary pupils across the land competed against each other to win the much-valued scholarship that would enable free entrance to a prestigious secondary school in the city. Many children from country areas who attended the city's secondary schools, boarded in the town during term time. "Boarding" had been a lucrative business for families who lived in large houses with one or two spare rooms. The Catholic Convent also provided a boarding facility for students. One of the lucky few who had worked hard to achieve his coveted scholarship originated from St David's. He reported that his family had been extremely proud of his accomplishment and that he was boarding with relatives who lived in St George's town when the *Island Queen* departed on her pleasure trip to St Vincent.

Indeed, the secondary education provided in Grenada at the time of the *Island Queen* excursion was deemed the best in the region. And children of the "well-to-do" from other islands in the region, such as St Vincent, St Lucia and Dominica, were educated in Grenada.

Those who held teaching positions in the island's secondary schools were of the highest calibre and were, in the main, selected from candidates who resided in Grenada, Carriacou or Petite Martinique.

All children attending elementary or secondary schools in the city were required to wear uniform. Secondary schools' uniform included distinctive ties and badges that were sewn onto the pockets of shirts or blouses, and Panama hats, trimmed with a band identical in colour and pattern to the school tie, were worn by girls. All secondary school pupils wore the obligatory leather shoes, accompanied by ankle socks. On the other hand, ties were never a part of the elementary school uniform and the footwear was usually white plimsolls, commonly known as "washekongs", that could be worn with or without white ankle socks.

The majority of children who attended fee-paying secondary schools were the offspring of comparatively well-to-do parents and in the city a child's economic background was often reflected in his or her school uniform. But there was also a "student-imposed" hierarchy in secondary schools for boys in relation to the length of "pants" worn by contemporaries. Essentially, boys who "sported" the more expensive long pants considered themselves "cool" and vastly superior to lesser mortals in "short pants".

In an era when there were relatively few cars on roads in the city, the sidewalks and narrow streets were playgrounds for the town's children. And pedestrians generally turned a blind eye and deaf ear to happy, screeching children as they skipped, played marbles, steered bicycle wheels or engaged in various hit-and-run or ball games. A gentleman who was just 14 years old at the time the *Island Queen* sailed recalled engaging in football and cricket with peers at a landmark grassy area of the town known as "Old Fort". The boys also played a game called "stick m up", modelled on "Cowboy and Indian" films shown at the local cinema and using sticks or planks of wood as replica guns.

Saturday was cinema day for many people who lived in the town at the time of the *Island Queen* excursion. The cinema which showed the latest American movie of the day was divided into three sections and graded in cost, the upper area or balcony offering the most expensive seats. There were afternoon and evening viewings and afternoon matinees were attended mainly by children. The lower level of the cinema, commonly known as the "Pit", was a dark area that was visited in the evenings not only by less well-off members of the community, but girls who were deemed free with their favours. And it was the section of the cinema also frequented by opportunistic young men intent on indulging in a bit of illicit slap, tickle and fondle with willing members of the opposite sex.

The environment within the small concrete city of St George's may have lacked the calm and serenity of unspoilt country areas. An individual of the era who lived in a country village described waking at around 5.30 am and being "spell-bound" by the rising sun as it scaled over hills and mountains in an increasingly bright glow. But sublime views of turquoise seas, the bright yellow ball that slid down the skyline and disappeared into the sea's horizon at sunset, and even the tranquillity derived on hearing the sound of pounding rain on galvanised roofs, were sublime moments for town and country folk alike. The Forte, a historical plateau situated at the top of a hill in the city, provided magnificent ocean scenery.

The "Botanical Gardens", with their well-maintained lawns, beautifully laid flower beds and tree-lined pathways, had been one of the most regularly visited parks in St George's. It was a tranquil and serene place of nature enjoyed by locals and where groups of nuns, dressed in white habits, ambled in silence as they "soaked up" the peaceful surroundings. At a time when the island was essentially void of modern technology, the majority lived comparatively simple lives; and spirituality, religious faith and an ingrained awareness of being at one with nature were powerful life-drivers.

The stillness of the Botanical Gardens was broken every other Sunday afternoon by the jolly sounds of the town's Police Band. Sunday had been the national day of rest or leisure, when families who resided in St George's town caught up with relatives and close friends. There were those who picnicked on the beach, but many visited the Botanical Gardens or The Forte, where on alternative Sunday afternoons they would be entertained by the Police Band.

The Botanical Gardens had also been the place where groups of young men and girls visited on Sunday afternoons with the primary intention of finding love. It was an age when it was the accepted norm that men were the initiators when forming relationships, and well-groomed young men wearing hats and dressed in their "Sunday best" blue double-breasted blazers adorned with brass buttons, white flannel "pants" and two-toned black and white shoes, would mooch past groups of self-conscious, giggling girls in fashionable dresses, buckled shoes and attractive hairstyles. The prospective suitors would discretely assess the beautiful "talent" before making a pre-calculated move on a fancied girl. It was without doubt that every young girl present secretly wished to be one of the "lucky" girls picked by a good-looking boy. It was, after all, their reason for being at the Botanical Gardens on that particular day and time.

A person's gender or sexuality was never an issue. As far as the majority was concerned, ambivalence did not exist, as a person's gender, male or female, was defined at birth. But rumour has it that the exception was a very popular woman in the town whose sexuality was secretly questioned by many. The individual reportedly wore three-quarter-length pants at all times and her mannerism, posture and swagger was "just like a man". The extraordinary "female" was at some point allegedly kidnapped in a prank carried out by a group of drunken visiting sailors. The young seamen apparently bundled the woman onto their ship, where they proceeded to pull down her pants and satisfy their curiosity, before releasing their terrified and bewildered victim. But a gentleman's decorum prevailed and the woman's true sexuality was never disclosed by the inquisitive, drunken sailors.

Unlike country areas where the population was reliably dependent on produce from the land, city folk had no option but to purchase food from the market or grocery stores and, as a consequence, a number of people who lived in St George's would have experienced relative poverty. The poorer or less qualified may be employed as store-hands, some form of factory or labouring job or servants to those who were relatively better off. But many proud and independent individuals refused to be servants to the elite and opted to do "trafficking". "Trafficking" was a small business venture which involved various commodities being bought and sold between Grenada and neighbouring islands.

Despite the class divide that was primarily based on family background, educational or occupational status or material possession, people were generally accepting of their lot in life and not envious of others, and everyone knew or knew of each other. The town community in which lived the majority of individuals on the *Island Queen* excursion consisted essentially of a friendly, respectful and laid-back diversity of people. The environment was lethargic. There was never a sense of hurry and the word "stress" was never used, or more than likely unheard of. Although there was on the whole very little decorum and blunt speaking had been the norm, it was in essence a compassionate and respectful community, and "good morning", "good afternoon" or "good night" had been the customary mutual greeting or term of acknowledgement.

The Impact of War

After being granted partial self-government by the British colonialists in 1763, Grenada returned to being a crown colony in 1877. It followed a vote taken in 1876, at the House of Representatives in St George's, to petition the Queen to make Grenada a Crown Colony. This meant that Britain controlled the affairs of Grenada and all laws for governing the island were debated on and passed in Britain. But a climate of grievance prevailed among the people, who had no constitutional rights regarding the manner in which they were being governed. In 1883 a campaign for self-determination was initiated and carried on by subsequent generations. The baton was passed to Theophilus Albert Marryshow, newspaper owner, editor and political writer, in 1915. Marryshow represented his generation in spearheading the campaign on behalf of the nation from 1915 with a broadened agenda. It incorporated a personal crusade for self-government and federation not only for Grenada but all British colonies in the region. The campaign culminated in 1921, when Marryshow boldly embarked on a lone mission to the Houses of Parliament in London, England, where he was granted the opportunity to present his arguments for self-determination. Marryshow's gallant initiative was positively received and resulted in Grenada and every other British Colony in the Caribbean being granted constitutional rights by the British Government to elect, at local level, their own government representative. Colonial power in the region was represented by a British Governor.

And so it was, in August 1944, when the *Island Queen* sailed on its pleasure journey to St Vincent, Crown Colony Government had been replaced with an elected government representative in each parish on the island of Grenada. Theophilus Albert Marryshow, politician and editor of *The West Indian*, the island's main newspaper, represented the town of St George's. He had been elected to the Legislature in 1925. The United Kingdom retained overall colonial rule.

At the outbreak of World War 2 in 1939, the Grenada Volunteer Force and Reserve, which had already been in place, joined with the Police Force under one Commanding Officer and became known as The Grenada Defence Force. The men of the Regiment received appropriate military training and were equipped with uniforms and rifles prior to taking up positions in defence of the island.

Patriotic young men, keen to actively defend the "mother country" by enlisting in the British Army, were advised by the Colonial Office to stay at home and seek to protect their own country, which could be at risk of German attack, by joining The Grenada Defence Force. Despite this advice, a number of young men travelled to Canada or the United Kingdom and were enlisted into their respective armed forces. Several would not return. An individual disclosed that his uncle joined up with the British Royal Air Force, but was lost after his aircraft was shot down. Various women of the time contributed to the war effort by knitting balaclavas, scarves, gloves and socks, which were donated to overseas troops.

Naval battles in Caribbean waters which began in 1941 escalated significantly during the years 1942 and 1944, and was a period when British and American tankers transporting bauxite, molasses and oil from refineries in the region to Europe and North America were being systematically obstructed by German U-boats and Italian submarines. The area was defended by American reconnaissance aircraft and British submarines and destroyers, and consequently involved both Allied and German ships being slammed into, attacked and sunk.

Coastal areas were also targeted and included the SS Oil Tanker *Sylvan Arrow* being torpedoed in the Caribbean Sea, south-west of Grenada on 20th May 1942. Subsequent repeated attempts to tow the tanker to port failed and she sank on 28th May 1942. This incident occurred two years before the schooner *Island Queen* embarked on her historical journey in 1944.

All the while, United States forces were actively defending the Panama Canal, the route taken by ships from Guyana carrying imported bauxite to the United States. The American military aircraft production had been crucially dependent on imports of the highly valued clay yielding aluminium from the South American British colony which at the time was known as "British Guiana".

German sailors who survived the hostilities were captured and made prisoners of war in the United States.

Caribbean involvement in World War 2 included a United Kingdom base at Piarco International Airport on the island of Trinidad; and the Dutch Caribbean islands of Aruba, Curaçao and Bonaire were occupied by British forces after the Netherlands was invaded by Germany in 1940. The occupying British troops were subsequently replaced by American troops in 1942.

Activities of war in the Caribbean and principally in Europe had been regularly reported in Grenadian newspapers and in particular the island's main journal, *The West Indian*. Reports of significant actions of war in Europe would have included the Battle of Britain in 1940 and ensuing German air raids over London; the invasion and occupation of 15 European countries, including France, Norway, Denmark, Poland, Italy and Greece, by German forces between 1939 and 1941; and the liberation of France by multi-national allied forces, including American, Australian, British, Canadian and New Zealanders that landed in Normandy, a town in southern France, on 6th June 1944. The highly successful operation was known as the D-Day Landings, and occurred just two months prior to the departure of the schooner *Island Queen* on her voyage of pleasure to the island of St Vincent in August of that year.

Meanwhile, Russia, which had been invaded by German troops in the summer of 1941, was at the time of the *Island Queen* excursion continuing its ferocious defence, which is estimated to have eventually cost the lives of more than 20 million Russians.

Significantly pertinent to World War 2 was the round-up and transportation of millions of European Jews to concentration camps such as Auschwitz in Poland. Men, women and children were persecuted, ill-treated and murdered. Other minorities, including homosexuals, people with learning or physical disabilities and non-whites, also suffered a similar fate. The snubbing of the black American athlete Jesse Owens at the Olympic Games held in Berlin in 1936 may have been indicative of a prevailing climate of bigotry. The then German Chancellor, Adolf Hitler, had refused to shake the hand of Owens, who won three gold medals at the Games. Hitler was alleged to have uttered words to the effect, "Do you think I would allow myself to be photographed shaking the hand of a nigger?"

Personal experiences of war on Grenadians, particularly those who resided in St George's, had been at times traumatising. Several who were children at the time reported being "terrified" on hearing the alarming sounds of sirens, followed by total blackouts. A young girl, who in war time lived with her family in the town, disclosed that on hearing the sirens, she and her siblings were instantly gripped by the fear that the island was under attack. Trembling and with bated breath and pounding hearts, the siblings would quickly take shelter by jumping into bed and disappearing under the sheets, hide inside wardrobes or cower underneath chairs, tables or beds.

But there were lighter moments, particularly for the young women who were both willing and happy to provide a service to visiting sailors. These attractive individuals would parade along the sea-front at night time dressed in revealing clothing as they pursued business with sexually needy passing seamen. The women were particularly excited in anticipation of getting their hands on "good money" when United States ships docked into the island's pier. An American Consulate had been located in close proximity to the sea-front and personnel from the United States regularly visited the island. American marines were well known for their generosity and at a time when the English pound was the national currency, the "yankee dollar" had been an attractive and highly valued alternative.

Among the consequences of war on the island of Grenada were shortages in imported items such as petrol, vehicle spare-parts, kerosene, matches, toiletries, salt and flour. Manufactured or imported food products, including cornflakes, porridge oats, granulated sugar, rice, English apples and Irish potatoes, had also been in short supply. These relatively expensive items had been, prior to the onset of World War 2, purchased and consumed by town folk, and in particular those from the "better off" section of the community.

An 11-year-old town resident of the period clearly remembers his family being among the majority in the community who had been given a "ration book" from the Government. The "little book" was presented when purchasing imported dried food such as rice or sugar. It ensured that no more than the permitted amount was being sold.

But the realities of war dictated that the only reliably available food options were the naturally sourced variety that had historically been satisfyingly ingested by the ordinary majority and in particular the people who lived in the countryside. These nutritional products, such as breadfruit, sweet potato, yams, cassava, corn and molasses, previously considered inferior by the affluent, were now being gratefully consumed by both rich and poor. Every fruit, vegetable or provision picked from trees or dug up from the ground was being fully exploited due to lack of choice.

The shortage of imported items resulted in large notices of "just arrived" items being featured in the newspapers. These items may have included ladies and gents' footwear, the much desired "trendy" Sky Scraper shirts of the day, various named brands of cigarettes, perfumes and health products, dried goods such as flour and rice, and edibles, including pickled fish. Everyone with money in their pockets would hurry to the named retail outlet, hoping to be one of the first to "snap up" the much-needed or desired item.

The prosperity of the island had been affected by a significant drop in the price of nutmeg and cocoa from 1938 until 1941. But, following the bombing of Pearl Harbor in December

1941, shipments of nutmeg from the Far East to Europe and America ceased. There was, as a consequence, a high demand for Grenada nutmeg: prices soared and a fortune was made by large nutmeg dealers and small stake-holders alike. This fact in no way impacted on individuals, particularly from the younger generation, who had been intent on seeking better economic opportunities in comparatively richer islands in the region such as Aruba, Curaçao and Trinidad.

Notwithstanding the various difficult experiences, there was essentially very little change in the lifestyle of Grenadians during the war years. Families continued to function, children attended school, everyone attended Church on Sunday, adults went out to work and business and public services were being maintained. Every opportunity for a good time was eagerly grasped and celebratory days, parties, picnics, sporting events, carnival, festivals and parades continued as normal. It was within this spirit in a time of war that an advertisement appeared in the *West Indian* newspaper approximately six weeks prior to the much-anticipated Emancipation holiday weekend. The advertisement indicated that an excursion of pleasure to St Vincent on the Auxiliary Schooner *Island Queen* would leave Grenada on Saturday, 5th August 1944 and return on Wednesday, 9th August 1944. Although a number of Grenadians of the era owned boats and various individuals regularly used a boat service for commuting between Grenada and other islands in the region, parties held on moving vessels were largely unheard of. And many people, particularly members of the younger generation who lived in the island's city, St George's, were captivated by the idea.

The dates of the August Bank Holiday weekend had been highlighted on the nation's calendar and the pleasure excursion on the schooner *Island Queen* was just one of a variety of organised activities planned for the fun-packed holiday weekend in August 1944. There was indeed a "national high" as people up and down the country looked forward to what was expected to be a long and enjoyable holiday break.

Saturday, 5th August 1944

At long last, the day that everyone was waiting for had finally arrived. It was Saturday, 5th August 1944; the holiday weekend was upon the nation and an intense "feel good" factor rippled throughout the land. Individuals in country areas up and down the island prepared with joyous enthusiasm for the various planned social, sporting or family activities that lay ahead. They involved the slaughtering of pigs and chickens, digging-up yams and sweet potatoes, picking and shelling peas, baking bread, cakes, puddings and candy in readiness for parties, picnics and family feasts. The people who resided in St George's made similar preparations, but obtained meat, poultry and provision from country traders. Those who for whatever reason did not do their own baking, purchased from local bakeries.

Young women all over the island had final fittings of newly made dresses, ironed garments, straightened and curled their hair with hot combs and curling tongs. Young men cut each other's hair, while their mothers, wives or partners ironed shirts and "pants". In preparation for entertaining revellers at organised party events, band members up and down the island rehearsed popular tunes on guitars, banjos, violins and drums. Sportsmen practised their skills in football or cricket in advance of competitive games scheduled to take place over the holiday weekend. The national athletics games that was held in August each year was advertised in bold, eye-catching letters in the *West Indian* newspaper. The popular and well attended games had been scheduled to take place in the town of Victoria on Monday, 7th August 1944.

Although they had been looking forward to participating in various social activities during the holiday weekend, ordinary people who lived in the town of St George's had been particularly aware of the party on the schooner *Island Queen* advertised six weeks previously and scheduled to begin on the afternoon of that very day, Saturday, 5th August 1944. It was a community where everybody knew everybody and their business and included the Captain of the schooner *Island Queen*. It had consequently been common knowledge that the Captain was also the owner of the pleasure schooner. He originated from Syria, but had been an established resident in the city of St George's for many years.

The Excursion Schooners

The *Island Queen* schooner was larger and heavier than the average Grenadian schooner. The vessel, constructed by local boat-builders in the town of St George's, was launched in June 1939. It had been during a period when boat-building had been a well-respected occupation and many Grenadians owned and captained boats that were commonly used for transporting passengers, livestock, various materials and goods, including fuel and foodstuff, to and from neighbouring islands such as Trinidad, St Vincent, Dominica and St Lucia.

Equipped with a powerful 125 horsepower German-made Krupps diesel engine and large capacity for transportation, the schooner *Island Queen* had been one of the busiest operational vessels of the time. The *Island Queen* was also known to provide the fastest service to and from the island of Trinidad. An 11-year-old female of the period vividly recalled travelling to Trinidad with family members on the schooner *Island Queen* just weeks prior to the pleasure excursion. The journey was reported to have been turbulent and "very shaky". The woman alleged that she was one of a number of passengers "throwing-up" on the deck floor. Nonetheless, the woman lavished praise on the crewmen for being attentive and most helpful. They did not hesitate in "cleaning up the mess", she said.

The owner of the *Island Queen* schooner also captained his ship. He was a "60-something" Syrian-born Grenadian national by the name of Chykra Salhab. He came to the Caribbean with his family when he was just a small boy and by the year 1944 had been a Grenadian resident for 37 years. Mr Salhab was a member of a sub-community consisting mainly of Syrian-born Grenadian nationals and their families who lived in St George's town. Many Syrian-born Grenadian nationals of the day had been highly successful business entrepreneurs in the island's capital.

The *Providence Mark* was the second schooner commissioned for the excursion. The vessel was built by local boat-builders in the parish of St Andrew's. She provided less capacity compared to the schooner *Island Queen*, but was considered appropriate for carrying the surplus number of people who sought tickets for the pleasure excursion on the primary schooner.

The *Providence Mark* had been a well-known schooner in the parish of St Andrew's and was regularly used for the transportation of local people as well as merchandise between the town of Grenville and the island of Trinidad. The schooner was owned and captained by a gentleman called Mark Hall. He was an experienced and respected seaman, who originated from Grenada and resided with his family in the town of Grenville, St Andrew's. Mr Hall was in his early forties when he took the helm of his schooner and sailed from Grenada to St Vincent on the Bank Holiday weekend of Saturday, 5th August 1944 with his consignment of holiday-makers.

The Excursion is under way 5th August 1944

The advertised pleasure excursion had been an unprecedented event. The population in St George's town had no memory of a previous similar activity taking place on their "door step". But even though the ordinary majority were excited by the prospect of an event that was accessible to everyone, they also knew that their inclusion had not been intended. And like various others across the social divide, they were not particularly interested. The disinterested individuals included not only those who were unable to afford the price of a ticket, but also persons who felt their money could be put to better use, such as the young, comparatively "well off" wife and mother who refused to fund the trip for her husband, a respected civil servant, from the family budget. Many had separate agendas and very much anticipated taking part in locally organised social activities with relatives and close friends.

A woman who, as a child, resided with her family on The Bungalow Housing Project revealed that various individuals in her particular community had been employed in a serving capacity by the Captain of the *Island Queen* and several others of similar social standing, and that "they" cooked on kerosene stoves and ate off china dishes with knives and forks while the people in her community cooked on coal pots, drank from pan cups and that their food was placed on aluminium plates and eaten with a single spoon. Despite being unable to afford to participate in the pleasure excursion, in reality Bungalow dwellers had no desire to mingle with "them" and were more than happy to be involved in their separate planned events or those attended by the ordinary majority.

In spite of the divisions that had been in place and associated with economic wealth or lack of it, work position, profession or educational status, the human connection that sustained the interdependent community could not be denied. Indeed, revellers who arrived at St George's harbour on 5th August 1944 to begin their journey of pleasure to Vincent on the schooner *Island Queen*, accompanied by relatives and friends, were joined by a large number of well-wishers from across the social divide; and many were from the nearby Bungalow project.

The schooner *Island Queen* had been scheduled to depart from St George's harbour at 1.00 pm on Saturday, 5th August 1944, but unforeseen circumstances came into play when a number of individuals with tickets to travel on the schooner *Providence Mark* stepped onto the party boat and stubbornly refused to budge. And what should have been a straightforward departure disintegrated into an intransigent melee. These persons included those who wished to journey with family members, peers, boyfriends or girlfriends; but a number of people were simply intent on having a good time with the beautiful girls on board. Essentially, every prospective reveller knew that if you really wanted "a piece of the action" you had to be on the party boat where "action" was guaranteed.

Personally invited relatives and close friends of the Captain of the pleasure vessel had been given priority of place. And it was stipulated that all minors should travel on the schooner *Island Queen* under the Captain's supervision. This impacted on the schooner's capacity to accommodate the unexpected high number of persons interested in purchasing tickets for the excursion and prompted the decision that a second schooner was necessary for carrying the surplus applicants. The vessel hired was called the *Providence Mark*.

Those who were at the pier to bid goodbye to relatives and friends looked on with curious interest, as impatient party-goers became increasingly frustrated as passengers holding tickets for the *Providence Mark* lodged themselves on the *Island Queen* and stubbornly refused to budge. All the while the Captain stood his ground. There could be no negotiation. He would not be sailing an overloaded ship. After several hours of futile pleadings, persuasion, debate and heated arguments, the situation was eventually resolved when individuals with tickets for the schooner *Island Queen*, anxious to get going, agreed to swap places with the protestors and transferred onto the schooner *Providence Mark*. These compromisers included all but one member of a football team known as "The All Blacks". The team had been scheduled to play a competitive match on the island of St Vincent that very weekend. Indeed, those who were successful in negotiating a much sought-after swap that guaranteed their participation on a journey that promised to be filled with jollifications, were ecstatic and considered themselves extremely "fortunate".

All passengers appeared delighted and relieved when the Captains of the separate schooners announced that departure was imminent. The *Island Queen*, with its 57 passengers and 10 crewmen, had been first to make her exit and within minutes was steering out of St George's harbour on a background of cathedral and church bells chiming the time of day and loud cheering and wolf-whistles from relatives, friends, well-wishers and ordinary bystanders. It was 6.00 pm on 5th August 1944. But the moment was suddenly and unexpectedly interrupted when, "out of the blue", a plucky risk-taker leapt from the *Providence Mark* and scrambled onto the deck of the *Island Queen*, while narrowly avoiding being short of the target and falling into the water. The inability to secure a swap did in no way deter the young fun-seeker from making sure that he did not miss out on a night of partying all the way to St Vincent. The startling and dramatic action had been momentary, and it was not too long before the beautiful and self-assured young passengers on board the schooner *Island Queen* had regained their composure.

There was not a cloud in sight to mar the brilliance of the clear blue skies on that gloriously sunny late afternoon of 5th August 1944. The radiant and beaming faces of privileged and jubilant fun-seekers with the world at their feet stood on the deck of the party schooner and waved furiously and ecstatically to relatives, friends and bystanders alike. It had been a "picture-perfect" transient moment in time. There was not an inkling of doubt in the minds of everyone present that the future that hovered on the horizon for these "lucky" young revellers was guaranteed to be as glorious as the day.

The *Island Queen* excursion to St Vincent had indeed been an unprecedented event of the era, not only in the little city of St George's, but throughout the island of Grenada. It could not have even entered the consciousness of any relative, friend, well-wisher or bystander who were at the pier on the afternoon of 5th August 1944 and witnessed the amazing departure of the excursion schooner *Island Queen*, that it was destined to be a pivotal and unforgettable experience, and a "red letter" day on the island's calendar.

As the *Island Queen* sailed from Grenada on her journey to St Vincent, raised voices and jovial singing of popular tunes played on guitars, violins and banjos resounded along the coastlines. And everyone who heard the jolly echoes had been reassured of the celebratory atmosphere on board. An individual, just four years old during the period, explained that, as the schooner *Island Queen* cruised, his uncle arrived at the pier, ticket in hand, only to discover that he had been left behind. In a fit of panic and anxiety, the young man hurriedly hired a rowing boat, which rushed him alongside the pleasure schooner and he was at that point hoisted on board. It had been a happy outcome for the eager and determined pleasure-seeker. He was elated to have caught up with the party schooner in the "nick of time". It would be an action of *fait accompli*.

Although the advertised party excursion had been accessible to everyone, there may have been passing feelings of jealously in the hearts of Individuals who witnessed the schooner as it cruised along the island's coastlines. These persons who harboured the desire to participate in the pleasure excursion may have been hampered by constraints such as financial difficulties. A child of the era who was raised on The Bungalow housing project in the town of St George's said that, even though various people in her community may have wished to participate in the excursion, they could not have afforded the ticket price "anyway". Indeed, the excursionists on the schooner *Island Queen* consisted mainly of the young and advantaged members of the better off, middle-class section of the local community.

Approximately 30 minutes after the *Island Queen* left the harbour, the second excursion vessel, the *Providence Mark*, left the harbour and began the parallel journey to St Vincent. Although passengers on the *Providence Mark* also waved happily to relatives, friends, well-wishers and ordinary bystanders, there was no display of excitement or exuberance. It had been, by comparison to the previous departure, a lack-lustre affair.

The angry and controversial scenes that resulted in the delayed departure of the excursion schooners, the movements of passengers from one boat to the next, the dramatic action taken by the young passenger who sprung from the

Providence Mark and onto the party schooner at the very last minute, and the chorus of applause that accompanied the pleasure schooner *Island Queen* as she eventually exited the pier with her beautiful and elite young passengers waving furiously and ecstatically to relatives, friends and well-wishers alike, had been somewhat of a side-show that had never been seen before at the St George's harbour. Consequently, the extraordinary string of unexpected events provided fodder for the sensational gossip that subsequently spread like wild-fire across the tiny city and beyond. Almost every person on the small island of Grenada had been aware of the unprecedented holiday excursion to the island of St Vincent on the schooner *Island Queen* which began on 5th August 1944. It had indeed been a phenomenal occasion.

In spite of the difficulties that occurred prior to the departure of the schooner *Island Queen*, the controversy was eventually satisfactorily resolved and the saying "All's well that ends well" was the common sentiment expressed.

News of the excursion to the island of St Vincent on the schooners *Island Queen* and *Providence Mark* appeared in *The West Indian* newspaper dated Saturday, 5th August 1944. Various other news items featured in *The West Indian* that day, related to recent activities of war reported under headlines including U-BOAT SUNK OFF AMERICAN COAST; MYITKYINA CAPTURED BY ALLIED FORCES; NAZI LEADERS MEET; and POLISH UNDERGROUND SEIZE WARSAW BUILDINGS. The departure of the *Island Queen* was featured under the headline: OVER 90 ON ST VINCENT EXCURSION. The article read: "An excursion party numbering 90 persons left for St

Vincent by two schooners last evening to spend the 3-day August holiday starting today. They are expected to return by Wednesday morning in time for work." The statement was followed by the listed names of passengers that had been scheduled to be on board the *Island Queen* schooner and also the *Providence Mark*.

How They Partied at Home

As the party boats sailed on their parallel journey to St Vincent, various families who lived in the town of St George's were meeting socially at each other's houses. Individuals "limed" by the roadside, while others congregated in "rum shops" or waited in line to view the weekend showings at the cinema. Movies being shown at the local "picture house" over the course of the holiday weekend included "Rage In Heaven", "Road To Morocco", "Who Is Hope Schwyter" and "Reap The Wild Wind". British World News was featured before or after the showing of each film.

Around 7.00 pm in the evening, young girls in St George's town and also across the island added the finishing touches to their hair and make-up and twirled in front of mirrors before heading off in groups to the various dance events that had been organised within their separate communities.

The women were allowed out on the condition that they chaperoned each other and would link arms as they walked along "shortcuts" to separate venues; and the air was filled with excited sounds of laughter and gaiety, inter-mingled with high-pitched expressions of feelings and desires in relation to particular boys they were hoping to dance with or even start a relationship with. At the same time, young men, "sporting" the much sought-after colourful and fashionable "skyscraper shirts" and with a few shillings jangling in their pockets, swaggered as they boasted with considerable bravado about separate females of interest they intended or rather hoped to "score" that night.

A woman who was just 19 years old at the time of the *Island Queen* excursion told of being among the selected guests at a party held in the local school-house of her country village on the evening of Saturday, 5th August 1944. She revealed that only those from "good" or "well-respected" families in the locality were invited and that the dress code was formal. The woman recalled being one of a number of attractively dressed young ladies being approached by equally appropriately attired young men, with hand outstretched, respectfully requesting "a dance"; and that boy and girl couples joyfully danced the "Castilian Waltz", the "Heel and Toe" or stepped in line for a formation dance called the "Quad-drill", in rhythm with tunes played on guitars, violins and banjos. It had been a memorable good-time occasion filled with laughter, gaiety and plenty of youthful exuberance.

The informant had been one of many young adults across the island mindful of arriving home no later than 10.00pm. Following an evening of partying, the island's youth accompanied each other on the way home. They ambled happily along in groups and in heightened voices punctuated by loud and hearty laughter, recounted the jollifications of the night. Those in newly initiated or ongoing relationships may have separated into pairs. In those days parents were generally very strict. A watchful eye was particularly kept on girls and if they were not home at the stipulated time, the late arrivals were usually picked up at some point on the return journey by a parent, grandparent or guardian with a freshly cut whip in hand, and the particular young girl would be systematically flogged as she was being marched all the way home. Alternatively, elders would wait patiently but angrily at the gate, strap in hand and poised to lash out at any late returner.

If a young female arrived home after the imposed time, the indiscretion, in those days, was judged to be "a bad sign" which indicated that the particular individual had been indulging in some form of immoral activity. It seemed inconceivable by largely suspicious elders that young girls, in particular, could be late on arrival home for any other reason. Interestingly, young men were generally exempted from blame, and any excuses, valid or not, were generally shouted down or totally dismissed. Crucially, the young party-goers of 5th August 1944 were expected to be home in good time on Saturday night to ensure sufficient rest to be fresh and alert for attending church on Sunday morning. The holiday weekend had in no way impacted on the fact that Sunday worship was a national "must". Indeed, joining with others in giving praise and thanks to the Almighty had been of primary importance.

As expected after a night of "jollies" on Bank Holiday Saturday, young and old throughout the land woke bright and early on Sunday morning; and men, women and children, dressed in their best outfits, set off with relatives and friends on the usual unhurried and, for the most part, silent walk to their separate church services. All the while church bells from the different Christian denominations, such as Catholic, Anglican and Methodist, chimed in unison, signifying the spiritual ambience of the morning. But the collective quiet mood disappeared at the end of the service and the return journey home was filled with laughter, chatter and the confirming of arrangements to "meet up" later that day. Church-goers, even in wartime, looked forward to being served the best breakfast of the week on returning home.

For individuals who lived in the town of St George's, sounds of joyful singing to a background of tambourines and beating drums filled the air in the market place and was, as usually the case, an irresistible draw to many individuals on their way home from church. Thoughts of breakfast would have been temporarily cast aside as they joined spectators and belted out well-known rhythmic spiritual songs in time with clapping hands and swinging hips. A woman who was just eight year old the time revealed that the weekly Salvation Army gathering had been, for her, a party event. She had no idea that it was actually a religious service! It was, indeed, a joyful and energising religious experience that was no doubt followed by a substantial breakfast spread on that memorable Bank Holiday Sunday morning in August 1944.

Scheduled activities on the second day of the holiday weekend in St George's town may have included a parade of marching bands in the market square, competitive sporting events such as football, cricket or netball and family picnics on the beach. A child of the time who lived in the community recalled her own family being, among others, equipped with the necessary ingredients for the "cook up" that had been organised to take place on a nearby popular beach in the town. It was alleged to have been a highly enjoyable afternoon of "fun" for the children with a lot of frolicking on the beach, swimming in the sea, and eating and drinking.

As people all over Grenada were having a good time during the holiday weekend, very little thought had been given to the "lucky" individuals on the party excursion. It was generally assumed that the holiday revellers had a wonderful journey, arrived safely at their destination, were happily spending quality time with relatives and friends, or had been engaging in a variety of social and sporting events on the island of St Vincent.

A Journey of Pleasure

While folk on the island of Grenada were participating in separate pleasure activities on Saturday, 5th August 1944, the schooners *Island Queen* and *Providence Mark* were steering a parallel journey on the 85.12-mile journey to the island of St Vincent. The schooner *Island Queen* followed a course further out to sea, while the *Providence Mark* sailed closer to the coastlines. The trip had been estimated to take between twelve and fifteen hours.

The party on the schooner *Island Queen*, which began soon after the vessel left the harbour at St George's, was in full swing. The ambience on board the schooner sparkled as effervescent young revellers cracked jokes, laughed heartily, chatted simultaneously in loud voices or sang gustily while dancing to popular tunes played by the band, the sounds of which were mostly "drowned out" by the noisy celebrations.

The schooner

It had indeed been a gleeful, uninhibited and romantic environment in which sweethearts embraced spontaneously and lovingly, and unattached boys and girls flirted light-heartedly with each other. All the while food and drink were readily available and freely consumed. The highly anticipated unprecedented pleasure excursion had surpassed all expectation.

Meanwhile, excursionists on the schooner *Providence Mark* were experiencing a pleasurable but, in comparison to the jollifications on the schooner *Island Queen*, more tranquil voyage to St Vincent. But excitement came into play as passengers on the schooner *Providence Mark* were suddenly gripped by a sense of competitiveness. They had spotted the schooner *Island Queen* in the distance and she appeared to be considerably ahead of their boat. Determined to "win the race", individuals on the *Providence Mark* not only urged the Captain to "step up" the speed, but gee-ed him along. Their efforts were rewarded when the schooner *Providence Mark* caught up with the pleasure vessel, which at that point could be seen in the distance. The passengers were jubilant, but the focus was now on overtaking the rival boat and they implored the Captain to go even faster. There was an ecstatic explosion of cheers, clapping and free-style dancing when, at approximately 10.00 pm on the night of Saturday, 5th 1944, the *Providence Mark* sailed past the primary vessel. The remarkable accomplishment was made "sweeter" by the fact that the *Providence Mark* initially trailed the schooner *Island Queen* by half an hour. It was indeed the highlight of what had previously been an essentially pleasant but uneventful journey.

Passengers on the schooner *Providence Mark* felt a sense of satisfaction as they settled down for the remainder of the night-long journey. Their vessel was now leading the "race" to St Vincent. It may have felt like being awarded a "consolation prize".

All the while, the party people on the schooner *Island Queen* may have been oblivious to the fact that their vessel had been overtaken by the schooner *Providence Mark*, but their concentration may have been solely on enjoyment. The revellers were indeed having the time of their lives. They had not a care in the world as they relished the carnival atmosphere. The good times just kept rolling on.

The pleasure schooner was for the last time spotted by various individuals on the schooner *Providence Mark* at around midnight on 5th/6th August 1944.

The Island of St Vincent

St Vincent is a beautiful and picturesque island in the Caribbean. It is a mountainous and volcanic land consisting of dense forests and rich plantations of bountiful varieties of tropical fruit and vegetables. St Vincent, which is 18 miles long and 11 miles wide, is separated from Grenada by a chain of islets known as The Grenadines.

The islands of Grenada and St Vincent had been long-standing trading partners in their separate natural resources and the peoples of both islands maintained a mutually friendly and respectful association. There were inter-marriages between the islanders and many children from privileged Vincentian families were educated in Grenada. A number of minors who travelled to St Vincent on the *Island Queen*, under the supervision of the boat's Captain, on Saturday, 5th August 1944, had been returning home for the holiday weekend.

Several of these children were accompanied by their Grenadian school friends, who had accepted the invitation to join them. It would no doubt have been an exciting prospect for the young invitees to be given the opportunity of spending the holiday period in a foreign country with close friends.

Crucial Days

At around 9.00 am on Sunday, 6th August 1944, when individuals throughout Grenada, Carriacou and Petite Martinique were attending church services, tucking into breakfast or preparing for planned afternoon activities, the schooner *Providence Mark* was docking into the harbour at Kingstown, St Vincent. It was the end of an overnight voyage which had taken approximately 15 hours. The passengers were not only relieved to have arrived safely but jubilant to discover the schooner *Island Queen* had not been successful in regaining the lead, and their vessel, *Providence Mark*, having arrived first, had achieved the goal of winning the race. Passengers, Captain and crew were delighted.

After disembarking their ship and being cleared through Customs, arrivals were greeted by various Vincentian relatives and friends who were gathered at the pier to meet them. Also at the pier were the relatives and friends waiting to welcome loved ones that were expected to arrive on the schooner *Island Queen*. Among them were the parents of children who were being educated in secondary schools on the island of Grenada. These children were returning home for the holidays and several were being accompanied by their Grenadian-born school friends.

Everyone present at the Kingstown harbour in St Vincent on that eventful Sunday morning of 6th August 1944 had been full of expectation. It was generally assumed that, in very little time, the schooner *Island Queen* and her exuberant passengers would be seen docking into port.

Within half an hour the majority of *Providence Mark* arrivals had collected their luggage and, accompanied by escorts, relatives or friends, had left the pier and were heading towards their final destination on the island. However, a number of arrivals decided to remain on the pier and wait for friends who were expected on the schooner *Island Queen*.

The small crowd who waited patiently and expectantly at Kingstown harbour, St Vincent, were in up-beat and optimistic mood as they looked forward to reuniting with friends and loved ones. Individuals related happily with each other and exchanged information regarding their separate plans for the holiday weekend. The atmosphere was filled with anticipation.

Meanwhile, the clock was steadily ticking. Seconds turned into minutes and within a heart beat the minutes had evolved into an hour. At that point any sense of disquiet that threatened to mar the shared optimism of the gathering was ignored. No one doubted that the schooner *Island Queen* and passengers would most certainly eventually make her appearance. The waiting crowd reassured each other that the schooner's delayed arrival would have been most probably due to bad weather or even engine problems. They remained confident in the knowledge that the ship's Captain, who also owned the vessel, had been a reputedly competent and experienced seaman.

The hand of time continued its rapid turn and in the blink of an eye pointed to 10.30 am. Ninety minutes had passed since the arrival of the *Providence Mark*, and there was still no show of the schooner *Island Queen*. It was the stage at which various individuals expressed feelings of anxiety and a collective decision was taken that the Vincentian Harbour Master should be informed of their growing concerns. The local police were afterwards alerted.

In response to being informed that the schooner *Island Queen* had failed to arrive within the expected time spectrum, the Vincentian authorities made contact by telephone with Grenada and Carriacou in their endeavour to determine whether the schooner had encountered difficulties en route and as a consequence might have returned to either island. Although it was affirmed that the schooner *Island Queen* had not returned to Grenada or Carriacou, the respective authorities were not seriously concerned. It was at that stage assumed that the schooner had drifted and would eventually make an appearance. Moreover, ships docking into port considerably later than expected had not been unusual during the period.

While many arrivals on the *Providence Mark* went on to participate in various pre-arranged activities on the island of St Vincent, there were those who refused to leave the pier and continued to wait alongside Vincentian individuals who were at the harbour to meet loved ones that were expected to arrive on the schooner *Island Queen*. No one at the pier in Kingstown, St Vincent, on the morning of Sunday, 6th August 1944, doubted that the party boat would be spotted approaching the harbour at any given moment, and imagined welcoming friends and loved ones with open arms, warm embraces and, most importantly, a huge sense of relief.

Feelings of apprehension or anxiety regarding the disturbing, unusual and unexpected prolonged late arrival of the schooner *Island Queen* were being stifled or swept under the carpet by the forever-hopefuls at Kingstown harbour, St Vincent, on Bank Holiday Sunday, 6th August 1944. At that same time, those who had chosen to engage in pre-arranged separate activities on the first day of the fun-packed holiday weekend found their enjoyment being marred by the uncertainty surrounding the unknown whereabouts of the schooner *Island Queen* and her passengers.

After a while the buoyant mood that existed at the harbour became increasingly subdued as time went on and there was still no sign of the expected vessel approaching. And relatives and friends were disappointed and deflated when they eventually went their separate ways, following a patiently long but futile wait for loved ones to arrive. Nonetheless, the shared view that the schooner *Island Queen* would most certainly, at some point, arrive at her destination, if she had not already returned to Grenada or docked into one or other port in the region, persisted.

Mid-day, Sunday, 6th August 1944 came and went, but there was still no sign of the schooner *Island Queen*. The pleasure schooner had left Grenada at approximately 6.00 pm the previous evening, 5th August, and headed out on an overnight journey of partying that should have lasted between 12 and 15 hours. But 19 hours had elapsed and she had still not arrived at her destination or any other port in the region. Concerns were now beginning to deepen and no more so than in Grenada.

In an initial endeavour to locate the vessel, the head of the British Fleet Air Arm based on the Island of Trinidad and the Hudson Motor Launches, based in the Grenadines, were alerted by the Grenadian authorities. The responses were immediate, but the requested air and sea searches revealed nothing. The skies were reported to be clear, the wind light and the sea calm. No distress signals had been picked up and nothing of interest that could be linked to any vessel was spotted.

Despite being troubled on receiving news of the delayed arrival of the schooner *Island Queen*, the relatives and friends of the vast majority of Grenadian passengers were not, at that point, unduly concerned, and, like many other people on the island, felt sure that the vessel and her passengers were somewhere in open sea, but safe nonetheless. They were confident in the belief that every effort would be made by the authorities in Grenada to find the vessel and that it was really only a matter of time before they were reunited with loved ones.

All the while rumours about the non-appearance of the schooner *Island Queen* were spreading, like wildfire, throughout the town community and beyond. It was sensational breaking news and individuals up and down the island were expressing personal opinions regarding the whereabouts of the missing schooner. It was, at that stage, generally believed that the missing vessel had drifted out to sea and would without doubt be eventually located. This nationally held conviction resulted in boat-owners from various parishes, sailing out to sea on personal missions to find the pleasure schooner. The well-intended separate endeavours proved fruitless.

There was, nonetheless, no shift in the national belief that the schooner *Island Queen* would at any moment be found drifting, eventually appear at the intended destination or another island-port in the region, or even arrive back home. Most importantly, relatives and friends of the missing passengers kept faith that all remained well and that sooner rather than later their loved ones would return to a joyful and heartfelt welcome.

Time moved on and with no reported signs of the missing schooner, a wave of speculative rumour emerged within the town community. In an environment where everybody knew everybody and everything that went on, it was not surprising that the people of the town had been fully aware of the pleasure excursion, and knew the vast majority of individuals on board the vessel. Indeed, many ordinary members of the town community were among well-wishers and bystanders who were at the sea-front on the afternoon of Saturday, 5th August and waved farewell as the schooner *Island Queen* began her pleasure journey to the island of St Vincent.

It had been a well-known fact within the town community that the schooner *Providence Mark* departed the pier at St George's at least 30 minutes after the schooner *Island Queen*. So, when news broke that the schooner *Providence Mark* had actually arrived at Kingstown harbour, St Vincent, at the expected time, it added a sensational element to the gossip and speculation that already existed regarding the missing schooner. But, despite the rumblings that "perked-up" the sluggish environment, the idea that the schooner *Island Queen* might have encountered some form of danger was not even entertained. And the nation as a whole shared the view of relatives and friends that the worst probability was that the pleasure schooner had lost direction and was simply waiting to be located.

The authorities in Grenada remained focused in their efforts to discover the whereabouts of the unaccounted-for schooner, *Island Queen*. Communication was kept up with the Royal Naval authorities on the island of Trinidad and updates of possible new developments in relation to requested search operations were at regular intervals requested. Progress reports were also required from authorities in neighbouring islands such as St Vincent, Barbados and St Lucia, as they too had been asked by the Grenadian authorities to undertake separate sea searches.

No positive feedback was received. Nothing of the missing schooner had been spotted. There remained not a thread of evidence that could throw light on the whereabouts of the schooner *Island Queen*, and elements of serious doubt and worry began to creep into the space previously occupied by optimistic expectation. It was the point at which the authorities in Grenada decided to step up the pace by initiating its own official search. The date was 7th August 1944, two days after the schooner *Island Queen* had embarked on her excursion of pleasure to the island of St Vincent.

It was war time and a Grenadian-owned schooner, christened the *Rose Marie*, had been modified and fitted with artillery for tackling U-boats by the United States Navy in readiness for service if and when required. The *Rose Marie* was now being loaded with food, water, fuel, first aid and ballast and placed on stand-by to be used, if necessary, for beginning the island's official search for the excursion schooner.

One of the strategies deployed by the Grenada authorities in finding the missing vessel involved the captain of every ship that docked into port at St George's harbour being interviewed by a designated Government officer. The questions asked had been tailored to determine whether any recollection of observations en route could throw some light on the possible location of the schooner *Island Queen*. The captains questioned were unable to provide any substantive evidence that could be used for assisting the search.

Intermittent repeated requests by the Grenada authorities for updated developments in searches being undertaken by Naval authorities on the neighbouring islands of Trinidad, Barbados, St Lucia and St Vincent revealed no new information. The whereabouts of the *Island Queen* continued to be a mystery. Where could she be? The missing schooner was now giving cause for grave concern, and was the stage at which the schooner *Rose Marie*, which had been appropriately equipped and placed on stand-by, was given the go-ahead to begin her search. The captain of the *Rose Marie* was directed to comb along the exact route that had been taken by the *Island Queen*. The schooner *Rose Marie* left Grenada, being the official search ordered by the authorities, at 6.30 pm on Monday, 7th August 1944.

The officially designated search that scoured the route to St Vincent that had been taken by the schooner *Island Queen* revealed no clues of the missing vessel. An alternative path scanned by the captain of the schooner *Rose Marie* on the return journey home also proved unsuccessful. The search vessel arrived back at Grenada at around 9.00 pm on Tuesday, 8th August 1944. The captain reported calm seas, light winds, clear blue skies, but, most crucially, absolutely no sightings. This was not news the Grenada authorities expected to hear. The red flags were, as a result, well and truly up and alarm bells began to ring.

While surveillance operations and air and sea searches were being maintained, Grenadian holiday-makers in St Vincent carried on – albeit with heavy hearts – with planned activities in which many individuals who had travelled on the schooner *Island Queen* were expected to participate. A particular event that went ahead as planned on the Monday was a wedding which should have been attended by several invitees who were among passengers on the missing schooner. But there was not one party-goer on the island of St Vincent on that unforgettable Bank Holiday weekend in August 1944 who did not believe that it was only a matter of time before the schooner *Island Queen* docked into port at Kingstown harbour, and that the late arrivals would be lovingly greeted by relatives and close friends.

Despite the unsuccessful outcome of search-and-rescue operations that had so far been conducted, there was no shift in the strongly held belief by Grenadian relatives and friends of passengers on the schooner *Island Queen*, and the people in general, that the missing vessel had been drifting somewhere in the ocean and would sooner or later be located, or most likely "put in" on the shores of an island in the region.

But three days had passed since the schooner was last seen at around midnight on Saturday, 5th August sailing en route to St Vincent. It was now Tuesday, 8th August, and with no reported sightings from ongoing air and sea explorations and surveillance, authorities in Grenada were becoming increasingly alarmed. Crisis meeting after crisis meeting was being convened by the Executive Council of the Government.

Having used all available resources in endeavours to locate the missing schooner and getting repeated negative results, the Grenadian Government arrived at the decision to seek the involvement of the Naval authorities in Trinidad for undertaking a wider and more extensive search of the area, both north and south of the region.

On the evening of Tuesday, 8th August, holiday-makers in St Vincent were boarding the schooner *Providence Mark* to begin their return journey home. Unaware of the rising anxiety in Grenada regarding the mystery surrounding the missing schooner *Island Queen* and the continuing official searches, the returnees were in buoyant mood and optimistic that they would soon be reunited with the absentee revellers who had travelled on the primary party vessel. It was generally felt among passengers on the schooner *Providence Mark* that the sister ship had experienced navigational difficulties which necessitated her return to Grenada. No one doubted that, as the vessel in which they were travelling approached the harbour in the town of St George's, the schooner *Island Queen* would become visible, having already moored into port. And happy optimism was shared by all.

For some relatives and close friends who lived on the island of Grenada, the swapping of tickets that had been negotiated between various passengers prior to the departure of both vessels resulted in a kind of self-imposed uncertainty. In particular, those whose loved ones had been known to hold tickets for travelling on the schooner *Providence Mark* hoped that they had been mistaken and that their particular relative or friend did not actually board the schooner *Island Queen* after tickets had been exchanged. But, despite the "wishful thinking", in reality the "doubtful" relatives and friends already knew the truth. They were present at the island's harbour on Saturday, 5th August 1944 and had witnessed the spectacular departure of the schooner of pleasure.

There were also relatives and close friends who may not have been at the pier on the day the holiday excursion began and were consequently genuinely unsure regarding exactly which of the two excursion vessels a particular loved one had taken for the journey.

And it was with heightened feelings of anxiety and ambiguity that relatives and close friends, with bated breath, waited to greet arrivals disembarking from the schooner *Providence Mark* at St George's harbour, Grenada, on the morning of Wednesday, 9th August 1944. Among the welcoming crowd were a large number of men, women and children standing along the length of the Carenage, the sea-front on which the harbour is situated. It reflected a community that was profoundly impacted by the unsolved mystery of the missing excursion schooner.

The Carenage

As the *Providence Mark* came into view and slowly docked into the harbour at 6.00 am on the morning of Wednesday, 9th August, the large waiting crowd surged forward. Everyone present had been eager to see exactly who would be disembarking from the vessel.

Relatives and close friends who had been waiting in anticipation to welcome loved ones were gripped by deep feelings of anxiety. Each person hoped their particular family member or contemporary would be among the arriving passengers. The suspense was intense and impenetrable. And, not surprisingly, many were relieved and overjoyed on being able to reaffirm that loved ones who originally booked to travel on the schooner *Island Queen* had indeed transferred onto to the schooner *Providence Mark* after swapping tickets. It was a proven fact that unleashed a euphoric roar of spontaneous and ecstatic screeches of relief, tears of joy, plentiful kisses and prolonged embraces.

It was, on the other hand, heartbreakingly disappointing for those whose relatives and friends were not among the arrivals. Their worst fears had been realised. The non-arrivals would have included *Providence Mark* ticket holders whose initial disgruntled mood had been transformed into delight after they had succeeded in securing the much-sought-after exchange agreement that provided the passport required for travelling on the priority excursion schooner. These particular individuals had been intent on enjoying a night of partying on the "good time" vessel all the way to the island of St Vincent.

The bona fide uncertain relatives and friends were also either happily relieved or deeply upset, depending on whether or not their loved ones had been among the arrivals.

All the while, the largely curious crowd looked on with hearts that were in equal parts of sympathetic and joyful.

Despite the contrasting and demonstrative expressions, the arrival of the *Providence Mark* for everyone present raised to the surface underlying grave concerns regarding the unknown location of the missing schooner *Island Queen* and her consignment of holiday-makers. It was without doubt an emotionally charged morning at St George's harbour, Grenada, on the morning of Wednesday, 9th August 1944.

With no information as yet in the offing, the people were keen to receive anything from the captain of the *Providence Mark* that might have thrown a little light on the possible location of the primary party vessel; and the captain was, as a consequence, bombarded with a variety of questions from relatives and close friends of the missing passengers on the schooner *Island Queen*. The questions included: At what time was the *Island Queen* last seen? What did he think may have happened to the vessel? Where might she be drifting now? And how was the weather? The captain explained that he had last seen the *Island Queen* at around midnight on 5th August. She had at that point been steering a parallel course, albeit further out at sea. He had no idea of her current position; but yes, the weather was fine on the night of 5th/6th August.

The holiday-makers who returned on the *Providence Mark* on Wednesday, 9th August 1944 were visibly disillusioned and dismayed that the *Island Queen* schooner had not already docked into port and that they would not be reunited with close friends and associates, as was previously so positively anticipated. The optimistic mood of expectation was now replaced with a deep sense of collective melancholy. The arrivals were also surprised on learning of the ongoing official air and sea searches and surveillance and that the entire nation had been praying for the safe return of her sons and daughters. But, like the vast majority on the island of Grenada, it remained inconceivable in the minds of the returnees that the missing schooner, with its illustrious cargo of beautiful, young people, could have come to harm. Hope was not abandoned, even though the party excursion that promised so much fun and pleasure had instead delivered considerable anguish to loved ones left behind.

Arrivals on the schooner *Providence Mark* had no choice but face the fact that, despite being weighed down by heavy hearts, the holiday weekend had come to an end and it was back to work at 8.00 am that very morning, Wednesday, 9th August 1944.

The overdue schooner had been the priority concern of the Grenada Government, and one of a series of meetings was held on the afternoon of 9th August by the Grenada Executive Council. Official search operations that had been undertaken to no avail were discussed and various additional measures that may be taken for intensifying ongoing operations were introduced and debated. Also on the agenda was the issue relating to sustenance. It was determined at the meeting that the schooner *Island Queen* was equipped with sufficient quantities of food and liquid for sustaining the passengers for one week, at least. The supply of subsistence carried by the vessel included 250lbs of vegetables, half a bag of flour and one barrel of biscuits.

As the nation waited anxiously for news of the long-awaited schooner *Island Queen*, the following headline appeared in the widely read *The West Indian* newspaper dated Thursday, 10th August 1944:

GRENADA EXCURSIONISTS OVERDUE. "Island Queen" Party Misses St Vincent Holiday Fiesta

News of the auxiliary schooner "Island Queen" has been eagerly awaited since she left St George's last Saturday evening for St Vincent with a party of excursionists.

The "Island Queen", with her crew of ten and 57 excursionists, left St George's at 6 pm and were followed by the "Providence Mark" with her party about half an hour later.

At about 9 pm the "Island Queen" was seen from the "Providence Mark" to be about 10 to 12 miles to the west. The latter vessel kept a course nearer land and was then about five miles off shore.

By midnight sight was lost of the "Island Queen", though a speck seen in the distance might have been her sails, but of this there could be no certainty.

The "Providence Mark" reached Kingstown, St Vincent, at 9 am Sunday and throughout the day the "Island Queen" was expected to turn up at any time.

The article went on to inform readers of the Government's response and action that had at that point been taken in endeavours to find the missing schooner. It included Government-commissioned air and sea searches and emergency meetings that had been convened.

A second report relating to the missing schooner under the headline "THE ISLAND QUEEN" had also been featured in *The West Indian* newspaper on Thursday, 10th August. Readers were advised against: "taking any pessimistic view as to the safety of those on board as incidents of the kind have by no means been uncommon. There are yet many features connected with the distressful occurrence which calls for uncompromising investigation, especially in view of the recent history of war-time happenings in our waters."

In response to rumours that had been circulating around the community, the article stated: "It would serve no useful purpose for Government to withhold any positive information, regardless of its nature, when any news of such an order is available." The newspaper urged "every citizen" to "refrain from indulgence in pessimistic rumour"; and readers were reminded that searches for "ship-wrecked seamen did not always result in immediate successes". In a final appeal to the mainly religious and God-fearing nation, it was concluded: "Patience, courage and a firm trust in the Almighty who rules the elements to which the missing are now exposed must be our present attitude".

The Mood of the People

The overall inclination of the people on the island of Grenada had been without doubt accurately captured in the aforementioned article, headlined "THE ISLAND QUEEN", featured in *The West Indian* newspaper on Thursday, 10th August 1944. It was indeed a period when rumour and speculation had been rife and in particular throughout the town community.

The town community of St George's was gripped by anxiety and restlessness, and the atmosphere was charged with tension. As the days dragged on and with still no definitive answers or reported sightings of anything significant that could offer clues into the mystery, various individuals may have felt compelled to come up with their own theories regarding the likely fate of the pleasure schooner. The speculation included:

1) The schooner *Island Queen* had been hijacked by a German submarine and re-routed to South America.
2) The vessel was captured by a German ship and the passengers were abandoned somewhere off the coast of Africa.
3) The missing schooner had been struck by a floating mine and exploded into smithereens.
4) It was rumoured also that the schooner *Island Queen* had been sucked underwater when it passed over "Kick 'em Jenny," the named undersea volcano that is situated en route between Grenada and the sister isle of Carriacou.

Sensational gossip was generated by the ever-increasing rumour and speculation that was bandied around the town of St George's and beyond. Many people were convinced that the Government knew a lot more than was being revealed and was holding back information, while a variety of personal opinions and views were being expressed. Each person was convinced that their very own calculated theory regarding the fate of the missing schooner had been the most probable.

A "tongue in cheek" but no less pessimistic rumour involved the alleged discovery of one of a pair of canvas shoes, commonly known as "washekongs", in the market square. The single shoe belonged apparently to a popular and charismatic ladies' man in the community, commonly known as a "saga boy". The individual was reportedly seen boarding the schooner *Island Queen* and on his feet was the particular footwear. The discovery of just one of the pair of shoes worn by the owner on boarding the vessel was considered a "mystical sign" which indicated that the popular "saga boy" had been claimed by the sea.

Despite the rumour and speculation, hope had not been abandoned. An 11-year-old of the era remembered clearly the almost daily message that was like wild-fire quickly spread throughout the town: "The *Island Queen* is coming!" "The *Island Queen* is coming!" The news would always be met with a collective sense of optimism and accelerated anticipation. The young girl claimed she was among many who sprinted to the pier with hearts bursting with expectation, only to be dashed. Time and time again the rumour that promised resolution would dissolve into feelings of dejection and bitter disappointment.

Various family members and close friends of the unaccounted-for excursion revellers supported each other in a daily vigil of many hours at the island's pier. Hopes would rise every time a vessel was spotted approaching, but hopeful hearts would sink to the deepest low when schooner after schooner could not be positively identified as being the long-awaited vessel. But spirits would once again be lifted as soon as yet another advancing boat came into view. Indeed, every approaching vessel was anticipated to be the schooner *Island Queen*, but initial stirrings of elation and relief were always short-lived. The whereabouts of the absentee schooner and loved ones on board remained a puzzle and the consequential emotional roller-coaster seemed endless. What has become of them may have been the all-consuming thought of every person who waited with expectant hearts at the pier. But hope was far from being lost. The waiting and watchful family members and close friends remained convinced that the schooner *Island Queen* and her passengers were safe, and their paramount wish was to be present at the pier to welcome loved ones on their return home. It was really only a "matter of time" had been the unanimous and unshakeable belief.

The disappearance of the schooner *Island Queen* occurred during an era when religion was considered essentially integral to the island's culture. Belief in Jesus being the Son of God the Father had been fundamental and everyone turned to prayer in times of difficulty. Prayer, they said "could move mountains". It was the basis on which prayer petitions and special services were offered in churches of every Christian denomination up and down the Island for the safe return of the schooner *Island Queen* and her passengers. Separate prayer meetings were also organised. These were usually conducted at the homes of specific volunteering individuals. And pupils in schools across the island were led by teachers in daily prayer for the missing excursionists. A woman who attended St Joseph's Convent revealed that two of her school friends and a teacher had been on the *Island Queen* excursion. She recalled "the Rosary" being said every morning prior to the beginning of lessons. It was repeated before the lunch break and finally prior to the end of the school day.

The outpouring of emotional expressions had been a measure of the climate of tense uncertainty and high anxiety that hung heavily within the small community of St George's. But rumour and conjecture continued unabated, despite the appeal that was made in the edition of *The West Indian* newspaper dated Thursday, 10th August 1944. The article stated: "We expect every citizen to do his or her part while the tension lasts by refraining from indulgence in pessimistic rumour, bearing in mind the many at home to be affected by such an attitude to the incident." The well-intentioned advice might not have been heeded by a significant number of individuals within the community who were caught up in the hype of rumour and conjecture; and with no definitive answers in the offing, from being curtailed, gathered momentum as time went on. It was a fact that in no way altered the climate of disquiet that weighed heavily within the community in St George's during the particular period of crisis.

All the while the relatives and close friends of the missing holiday-makers were encouraged by the ongoing air and sea rescue or recovery operations, even though the repeatedly unsuccessful outcomes were worrying. But "not knowing" what had actually happened to loved ones or where they might be located was of particular concern. However, comfort and strength were being derived from the prayers of the nation and the love and support of relatives and close friends.

There had been no united family-led private endeavours in finding the missing schooner and/or passengers, but individual family members consulted with well-known local clairvoyants and those whose dream forecasts had been proven to be reliable. Indeed, dreams and their related interpretations had been integral to the island's culture. These so-called "good" or "bad" dreams were believed to carry significant meanings and were thought to be correctly predictive of future events.

Spirits were raised when families received assurances from so-called dream experts that a particular dream had indicated the position of the missing schooner and wealthy relatives were persuaded to fund a privately commissioned sea search. The search involved the combing of the specified area of sea and adjacent coastlines, and local residents were asked specific questions regarding the missing schooner.

The privately financed endeavour unfortunately drew a depressing blank. There were no sightings of the missing schooner, nor was any debris, baggage or floating objects that could be linked to the vessel or her passengers recovered. The people interviewed were unable to cast light on the mystery. They had seen or heard nothing. The missing schooner had not moored along their coastlines, foreign persons had not landed, bodies or objects had not been washed up on their shores or been observed floating on the water. The much-anticipated investigation resulted in yet another crushingly disappointing blow for the relatives and friends of the missing holiday-makers.

While the gossipers were in full flow and the silent majority prayed and the waiting families struggled with their agonising emotions, the newspapers maintained a campaign of positivity that was designed to keep alive the shared hopes of relatives, friends and an entire nation.

Extracts taken from an article printed in *The West Indian* dated Thursday, 18th August 1944 under the headline:

"ISLAND QUEEN" PARTY'S ORDEAL NOT UNCOMMON

Absence of news of the "Island Queen" should not daunt the island-wide spirit of hope that the schooner's fifty-seven passengers and ten crewmen are yet safe.

As we have said earlier, other vessels have been missing for longer periods because wind, wave and tide are fickle elements, having counterparts in the air above which still baffles those who cleave the sky in aircraft despite all the technical aids modern science has provided.

On the "Island Queen" fortunately are quite a few older heads who, with Captain Salhab, can maintain morale and they have undoubtedly arrived at a judicious plan of rationing of supplies.

It was speculated in *The West Indian* on 17th August 1944 that:

The "Island Queen", now 10 days overdue, is most likely to be approaching a port either on a mainland coast or the closely set islands which enclose the Caribbean."

On 18th August 1944, *The West Indian* newspaper reported:

The still overdue "Island Queen" and its passengers were remembered before God in all churches of the colony last Sunday. It was but human that the emotions of not a few worshippers should have been uncontrollable. ... Leave everything in the hands of God rather than to share in the spate of rumours now abroad, despite the knowledge that the Administration waits on the verdict of another.

The anguish, pain and distress felt by the relatives and friends of the missing party had been accurately documented in *The West Indian* and witnessed during a church service attended by a 19-year-old young lady of the period. The woman recalled a heartbreaking outpouring of emotions and loud and uncontrollable sobbing by relatives and close friends of the missing holiday-makers, and that the congregation consisting of men, women and children had been reduced to sympathetic tears. "There was not a dry eye in the church that Sunday morning," she said.

But while *The West Indian* newspaper continued to print messages of hope, a school boy of the era, whose father had been among revellers on the schooner *Island Queen*, said that he had been consumed by an unshakeable sense of foreboding. The boy just knew that the much-loved parent would not be "coming back home". He wept uncontrollably. It was approximately two weeks after the beginning of the holiday excursion. The young lad was also at that time sensitive to the anxiety felt by his mother and the tense atmosphere within the family home, but the children received no explanation regarding their father's unusually lengthy absence. Interestingly, the young wife and mother had expressed doubts about what appeared to be a pressing desire by her husband to participate on the excursion and refused to fund the trip from the family's budget. But her pleas were ignored and the young husband and father of three turned to his very own mother for the money required for purchasing the ticket that ensured his place on the party schooner.

Search and Surveillance

All the while, air and searches were continuing. The operations included scouring for wreckage off the coastlines of the Grenadines by a British ship and also a War Department vessel named the *El Alamein* on 12th August. Air surveillance was also ongoing and indicated by intermittent sounds of aircraft being heard above the town of St George's.

On 14th August, air and sea searches and surveillance were extended to cover the whole of the eastern Caribbean as far west as the Meridian of 71 West.

Further operations scheduled between 16th and 18th August were suspended due to hurricane winds sweeping across the specified area.

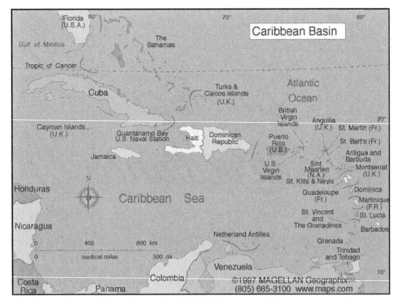

Map

Search and rescue or recovery missions were resumed on 19th August, with a close exploration of Avis Island, west of Dominica, but nothing of significance was detected.

A special search of the island of Blanquilla was conducted on 21ˢᵗ and 22nd August by United States aircraft. The action had been taken in response to a telegram request to the British Naval authorities based on the island of Trinidad from the Administrator of Grenada. The Grenadian Administrator asked for an examination into an unconfirmed report that an unidentified vessel had been spotted lying off the island of Blanquilla, north of Margarita. The investigation involved the co-operation of the Venezuelan authorities, who were required to keep a look-out for survivors landing on their northern coast.

Information regarding the spotted unidentified vessel lifted the hopes of Grenadian administrators. It seemed that the long-overdue schooner might have at last been located and everyone was cautiously optimistic. But the requested special search delivered no evidence of an unidentified vessel being docked off the coast of Blanquilla. Investigations carried out by authorities in Venezuela revealed no sightings of survivors on the country's northern coastline. It was back to the drawing board. The authorities were baffled.

Twenty-two days of official undertakings, initiated on Sunday, 6th August 1944 when the schooner *Island Queen* was reported missing, had produced no definitive clue that could be used for locating the vessel and her passengers. The authorities found themselves at a dead end. All scientific resources that were available during the period had been utilised in carrying out extensive air and sea searches and rescue or recovery endeavours. And with no sightings of wreckage, debris, lifeboats, pieces of luggage, items of clothing, floating bodies or indeed any form of evidence that could point to the probable fate of the pleasure schooner and her passengers, search teams were left mystified and at a loss regarding what else could be done. Every possible avenue explored revealed nothing. But how or why could a pleasure schooner filled with passengers simply vanish from the sea? The question, at that point, remained unanswered.

Reaction in St Vincent

During the period that the schooner *Island Queen* embarked on her journey of pleasure, St Vincent and Grenada were trading partners and the islands were mutually respectful of each other's culture and way of life. The harmonious connection resulted in romantic partnerships and intermarriage between men and women from St Vincent and Grenada being common place. Regardless of whether these mixed couples decided to settle on the island of St Vincent or Grenada, contact with respective relatives and friends was always maintained, and various children from "well to do" Vincentian families who were educated on the island of Grenada stayed at the homes of relatives or close family friends who lived in the island's city, St George's, during the school term.

In articles featured in Grenada's main newspaper of the era, *The West Indian*, dated 18th and 19th August 1944,

"Vincentians" were described as being "hospitable people of our sister colony"; and in relation to the absent holiday-makers, it stated: "Kingstown's air of festivity was distinctly spoilt, both for Vincentians who looked forward to a Monday holiday of sport and the Grenada visitors, who awaited the remainder of their party, some of them guests for a wedding at the Kingstown Cathedral."

Indeed, the particular wedding went ahead as arranged on Monday, 7th August 1944, in spite of the absent Grenadian invitees. It had been generally believed, at that point, on the island of St Vincent, that the schooner *Island Queen* and her passengers were safe, even though the vessel had so far not yet docked into Kingstown's port.

The wedding was subsequently reported in the *Vincentian* newspaper dated Saturday, 12th August 1944. Under the headline "WEDDING BELLS", it was stated:

> On Monday afternoon there was a pretty little wedding at St George's Cathedral when Kathleen Ianthe, daughter of Mr and Mrs O. C. Cruikshank of Kingstown was given in marriage to Mr George Donald Shearman.
>
> The *Vincentian* joins in wishing the couple a happy married life.

The parents of school children who were returning home for the holiday weekend and relatives and close friends of St Vincent-born individuals who were also expected to arrive on the schooner *Island Queen* had been aware of the ongoing official searches and surveillance being conducted in endeavours to find the missing vessel. But, in spite of the unresolved and increasingly worrying situation, loved ones on the island of St Vincent held on to the belief that the missing schooner would eventually be located and that there would be a happy outcome.

Apart from Vincentian involvement in the various search operations that were being undertaken, relatives and friends of the missing holiday-makers visited Kingstown harbour on a daily basis. It was with the expectation of witnessing the arrival of the schooner *Island Queen* and being reunited with loved ones. Various individuals who lived locally also kept a watchful eye on the harbour. Prayers were offered privately and in churches across the island of St Vincent for the safe return of the schooner and her passengers. But, as time went on and still no sightings of the missing schooner, levels of anxiety were being raised. In particular, the relatives and close friends of the unaccounted-for loved ones were profoundly distressed. One father's anguish was reflected in a column printed in the *Vincentian* newspaper dated Tuesday, 29th August 1944:

FATHER OF MISSING GIRLS VERY ILL

The Hon'ble A. M. Fraser, of Rutland Vale Estate, is seriously ill with high blood pressure. His illness has been accelerated by anxiety for his missing daughters, Jean and Patsy, who were aboard the ill-fated *Island Queen*, missing at sea since Saturday, 5th August. The Fraser sisters attended the Convent School in Grenada and took the schooner to St Vincent for their holidays.

Whilst holding to the hope of a happy ending, it was at the same time an agonising period for relatives and friends in St Vincent, Grenada and other islands in the region, as they waited to hear news of the missing schooner and loved ones on board.

The Search is Called Off

The rumours and speculation in relation to a schooner which was long overdue in making an appearance in no way eased the underlying "edginess" that lingered within the community. The continued unsuccessful attempts to find the pleasure schooner *Island Queen* had been a perplexing dilemma never before experienced and the people were bewildered. But Faith was their rock and hope reigned supreme. The nation remained confident that if the missing vessel was not found, she would at some point, most certainly, navigate her way back home. Life went on as usual and, in the town of St George's, businesses operated, children attended school or played on narrow streets and pavements. City workers, students, visitors and vendors from country areas exited with sighs of relief from cramped buses on arrival at the market square. Crumpled garments were smoothed by individuals before setting off on their separate daily activity.

And the hustle and bustle of the vibrant little city continued unabated under the intense heat of blinding sunshine that showed little mercy on profusely sweating brows.

The Grenada people were being provided with updated information by *The West Indian* newspaper of air and search operations that were being conducted. The printed messages were encouraging, uplifting and biblical. Placing everything in "the hands of the Almighty" seemed to be the bottom line of every newspaper article.

Three weeks after the initiation of official searches, the Naval authorities were at an impasse. Every technological resource available had been utilised for carrying out extensive search endeavours, but these missions proved unsuccessful again and again. Although all avenues explored had arrived at a dead end, it was nonetheless decided that surveillance of specific areas would continue.

Information relating to the various unsuccessful search operations and surveillance and the officers' views on the serious matter of the vanished schooner *Island Queen* were communicated to the Governor of the Windward Islands, Sir A. Grimble, in a telegram dated 22nd August 1944.

Governor Grimble's assessed response and presumed conclusion regarding the fate of the missing schooner and passengers were outlined in a memorandum dated 24th August 1944. The telegram, addressed to the Secretary of State for the Colonies, Oliver Stanley, was "repeated" to Senior British Naval Officer, Trinidad, No. 478; The Governor of Trinidad, No. 481; the British Minister at Caracas, No. 479; and the British Consul, Curaçao, No. 480.

1. Schooner ISLAND QUEEN 65 tons Grenada Registry, left Grenada about 6 p.m. Saturday 5th August with excursion party of 55 persons (34 women 21 males) and 10 crew for neighbouring island of St. Vincent as expected on morning of 6th August, and has not yet been seen since departure from Grenada.

2. First intimation that ISLAND QUEEN was overdue was received by me on 6th August in message from Grenada, when the assistance of the British and American naval authorities in Trinidad Command was enlisted in an extensive search of the Caribbean area and waters adjacent to the Venezuelan coast. A very thorough search has been conducted and I must place on record an expression of my gratitude for and high appreciation of, the ready and willing assistance, full cooperation, and advice which have been accorded to this Administration by the S.B.N.O. Trinidad, the American Naval Authorities, the Government of Trinidad, the British Minister at Caracas, and the British Consul at Curaçao.

3. On the 13th August, I despatched the following message to the people of Grenada and St. Vincent: "Please now assure Executive Council and local press of my deep concern for the ISLAND QUEEN, and my continuing sympathy with all those connected with Vincentian and Grenadian passengers on board from my first receipt of the news on 6th August." This was followed by the

following message which I addressed to the two Colonies on 21st August:

> "Though I am far from having lost hope for the safety of the ISLAND QUEEN, I nevertheless cannot refrain from conveying now to all those who have relations and friends aboard her, the assurance of my heartfelt and constant sympathy in the hours of anguished suspense through which they are passing."

4. A hope, though slender, for information concerning the missing vessel was conveyed to me in a telegram which I had received on the 21st August from British Naval Authorities at Trinidad to investigate an unconfirmed report that an unidentified vessel was lying at anchor off the island of Blanquilla, North of Margarita.

5. The British Naval Authorities Trinidad promptly instituted the investigations sought by Grenada, and I repeat hereunder for your information his latest report in a telegram dated 23rd August.

> "Your telegram, ISLAND QUEEN 22nd August confirmed that sailing vessel reported in your telegram of 21st was not (repeat not) ISLAND QUEEN, and search off Blanquilla produced negative results. Every possible step to find ISLAND QUEEN has been taken, and surveillance of area continues. It must however be realised that in views of time elapsed and very thorough search conducted the chance of getting news of vessel is now remote. (2) Word

would be quickly received if survivors had landed on Margarita Island. (3) As previously stated all adjacent shore lines have been and still are subject to close scrutiny from the air. It is considered additional naval surface craft for this work would be unavailing without prior specific information."

6. In view of the advice tendered above that "the chance of getting news of the vessel is now remote", I must, with deepest regret, come to the conclusion that the schooner ISLAND QUEEN must now be presumed lost with all hands on board. Neither survivors nor wreckage have been sighted on any of the searches.

7. In these circumstances I wish to send a message of sympathy to the people of Grenada and St Vincent who have lost relations and friends on the missing vessel.

8. I should be grateful if you would consider sending direct, or be good enough to authorise me to convey on your behalf, an expression of your thanks to each of the officers who are mentioned in my paragraph 2 above for the help and ready assistance which they all gave to this Administration in the search for the schooner ISLAND QUEEN.

9. I propose to cause the usual statutory enquiry concerning ISLAND QUEEN to be held and will report to you further should any developments materialise from the surveillance of the area and scrutiny from the air of shore-lines which continue as stated in S.B.N.O. Trinidad's telegram quoted in my paragraph 5 above.

In response to the telegram sent to the Secretary of State for the Colonies, Sir Oliver Stanley, from the Governor of the Windward Islands, Sir A. Grimble, dated 24th August 1944, regarding the presumed fate of the *Island Queen* schooner, a personal reply from Sir Oliver Stanley was despatched on 25th August.

The reply telegram stated:

> I have learnt with greatest regret news that schooner ISLAND QUEEN must be presumed lost with all hands and desire that you will convey my sincere sympathy to people of Grenada and St Vincent who must be presumed to have lost relations and friends on the vessel.
>
> I am very grateful for the efforts made by each and all of Officers referred to in paragraph 2 of your telegram, and shall be obliged if you will so inform them.
>
> I am bringing the services they have rendered to the notice of the Admiralty and Foreign Office.

The telegram sent to Sir A. Grimble, Governor of the Windward Islands, from the Secretary of State of the Colonies, Oliver Stanley, indicated that Governor Grimble's considerations and presumed conclusion regarding the fate of the schooner *Island Queen* and all hands on board had been accepted by the British.

Reaction to News Most Feared

The Governor's conclusion into the presumed fate of the missing *Island Queen* schooner and all on board made headline news in the *Vincentian* newspaper dated Saturday, 2nd September 1944.

It was the conclusion most feared by the people of St Vincent and also Grenada. Both nations were deeply affected.

The grim breaking news resulted in a deluge of messages of condolence to relatives from governments and ordinary sympathisers across the Caribbean, and many such messages appeared in newspapers on the island of St Vincent and also Grenada.

When Governor Grimble's summarised conclusion on the fate of the *Island Queen* and all hands on board became common knowledge in Grenada, the nation was shaken to its very foundation and shockwaves cascaded throughout the land. It had, at the time, been the most widely impactful catastrophe that had ever visited the island's shores. The population was stunned and profoundly saddened.

For relatives and close friends of loved ones presumed lost at sea, the most dreaded of news struck like a dagger through the heart. But despite being traumatised and totally broken, surviving loved ones did not lose their Faith in God or ask "why me?" They were instead even more dependent on prayer for strength and courage to help them through the devastating and overwhelming crisis.

Despite the failure of repeated searches and surveillance, much faith had been placed on the power of prayer and in Grenada the entire nation prayed diligently for the safe return of the schooner *Island Queen* and all on board. During the period of ongoing missions and surveillance in search of the excursion schooner and missing holiday-makers, the spirits of relatives, close friends and the people at large had been lifted and championed by continuous positive messages in Grenada's main newspaper, *The West Indian*.

On 13th August 1944, the newspaper stated:

> Absence of news of the *Island Queen* up to last evening should not daunt the island-wide spirit of hope that the schooner's fifty-six passengers and eleven crewmen are yet safe.

It was further reported on 17th August 1944 that:

> The *Island Queen* schooner had been 10 days overdue but was now most likely to be approaching either a mainland coastline or the closely set islands which enclose the Caribbean.

On 18th August, *The West Indian* newspaper informed its readers:

> Over the week-end further assurances were given to the local Government by the Caribbean Air Command that, although there is nothing yet to report, the search is still being continued with the utmost intensity. Of this we have daily evidence in the passing of aircraft whose temporary appearance is not simply intended to tell us they are still on the job.

But the national spirit of hope that had been so conscientiously nurtured in prayer and optimistically sustained by positive reporting in *The West Indian* newspaper was now brutally crushed by the Governor's devastating conclusion on the presumed fate of the missing schooner and all hands on board. The entire nation was left shell-shocked and caught up in a collective feeling of numbness and disbelief. Most importantly, the relatives and friends of those presumed lost at sea were totally broken and many struggled to absorb the tragic and traumatic news. There were those who went into denial mode. The harshness of the Governor's conclusion might have been too painful for some to accept and they would remain forever hopeful that their loved ones would one day return home. It may also have been thought inconceivable that such privileged and illustrious young, beautiful and beloved family members in the prime of their life and on the cusp of a bright and promising future could have been so unexpectedly taken.

Notwithstanding the rumours that flew around the small community in the town of St George's, in which lived the majority of exuberant revellers on the doomed schooner, there remained the underlying belief that no real harm had been encountered; and many members of the community prayed fervently for the safe return of the vessel and everyone on board. They were confident that sooner or later the schooner *Island Queen* would be spotted approaching the town's harbour to a chorus of triumphant fanfare. Even those who may have secretly feared the worst, prayed for a miracle. So when the reality of the news hit, the community trembled. A dark cloud descended and the little city of St George's was engulfed in an atmosphere of gloom and eerie silence. A woman who was just 19 years old at the time said: "The whole town went dead. None of the shops opened that day, the schools closed and children were sent home. It was terrible." The unofficial day of mourning had been independently imposed by separate public and private concerns in response to the sombre news.

Those who had witnessed the euphoric departure of the pleasure schooner *Island Queen* on that glorious evening of Saturday, 5th August 1944 relived the extraordinary moment. The picture-perfect images of joyful and radiant young party-goers with the world seemingly at their feet would rewind over and over again in the thoughts of many who were at St George's pier on that fateful day. The fact that destiny determined it to be the last farewell of the beautiful excursionists was met with complete and utter disbelief.

How "lucky" these confident and advantageous young people may have felt to be embarking on such a wonderful and once-in-a-life-time adventure of fun; in particular, those who arrived at the pier with tickets to travel on the *Providence Mark* but had been "fortunate" in successfully negotiating highly desired swaps which secured their place on the much-favoured "good-time" schooner. Not to mention the young man who refused to be flailed by being unable to negotiate a swap. He would demonstrate his resolve by suddenly and unexpectedly leaping from the *Providence Mark* onto the *Island Queen*. The particular individual was alleged to have, in the process, narrowly avoided slipping into the sea as he scrambled on board the vessel as she steered from the harbour; and, of course, the late-comer whose determination to be on the pleasure schooner for which he held a ticket prompted the panicked hiring of a small fishing boat, whose owner was instructed to row at speed in order to "catch up" with the party schooner. There could be no doubting the intense feeling of elation that was felt by the "nearly didn't make it" reveller as he eventually jumped onto the deck of the vessel that promised a "not-to-be-missed" night-time cruise filled with singing, dancing, eating, drinking and general merry-making, all the way to the island of St Vincent.

Individuals who were among well-wishers that participated in the celebratory departure of the schooner *Island Queen* may also have recalled the comparatively lack-lustre exit of the schooner *Providence Mark* on her parallel journey some 30 minutes afterwards. But the expressions on the faces of passengers who waved to reciprocating relatives, friends, well-wishers and ordinary bystanders at the waterfront, suggested that *Providence Mark* passengers had been relieved to be – at long last – starting out on a holiday break they had been very much looking forward to.

The delayed departure had been caused by original *Providence Mark* ticket holders who demonstrated their desire to travel on the *Island Queen* schooner by staging a "stand in" on the preferred vessel. Those who had conceded a swap appeared content in their decision and may have been resigned to a quieter and more restful experience, rather than the initially anticipated journey of partying and noisy jollifications.

A large number of people who were at the pier on the day the *Island Queen* sailed had been ordinary folk who could only dream of being able to afford the price of a ticket required for the pleasure trip on the schooner *Island Queen*, and there were several among them who could not help but feel a tinge of envy on that memorable day in August 1944 as they stood and watched the "privileged" embark on an excursion which appeared to cater exclusively for the beautiful and elite members of the then society. These disadvantaged onlookers knew instinctively that they would never be wholeheartedly accepted in "their club". It was at the time very much an "us" and "them" society. Even so, the poor were essentially content with their lot in life and were more than happy to participate in social activities with kindred spirits. This reality in no way impacted on the shared sense of grief that was felt by the community at large on hearing the tragic news. But the financially disadvantaged who had seen the glow of excitement on the faces of the excursionists as they embarked on their voyage of pleasure had been awestruck that the celebrated party revellers had all been claimed by the sea!

There are, as always, exceptions to every rule and various individuals among the ordinary majority harboured genuine doubts, and may have presumed that the radiant party-goers who stood on the deck of the pleasure schooner and waved furiously and joyfully to relatives, friends and well-wishers alike at St George's harbour on Saturday, 5th August 1944 had been much too beautiful, too privileged, too young or even too popular to have perished.

But social barriers that had been linked to a person's profession, wealth, success, race or skin colour had been shaken to their very foundations. Egos bowed as the equality of the human soul and spirit transcended the social divide. Rich and poor alike within the community experienced identical feelings of despair and sorrow at the loss of so many of the island's sons and daughters. It had indeed been a moment of humble awakening to the meaningful privileges that only God can bestow.

The people turned to God. Requiem services were held in churches of different Christian denominations up and down the island of Grenada. Candle-light vigils and prayer meetings were held. Special prayers for the souls of the lost individuals were offered in schools across the land, and numerous persons with personal messages of condolence and carrying gifts visited the family homes of loved ones lost.

The detailed background information contained in Governor Grimble's report that related to the schooner *Island Queen*'s voyage to St Vincent, his account of the various extensive but unsuccessful search operations that had been taken in repeated endeavours to locate and rescue the vessel and her passengers, and his overall assessment and conclusive summary on the presumed tragic fate of the schooner *Island Queen* and all hands on board had undoubtedly been the most dreaded, chilling news for the Grenadian and Vincentian relatives and close friends of the beloved lost souls.

The names of the 56 passengers and 11 crewmen on the vanished schooner *Island Queen* were printed in Grenada's main newspaper, *The West Indian*. The ages of the lost passengers ranged from 14 to 60-plus. The vast majority of passengers were in their late teens and twenties and resided on the Island of Grenada. The tragedy occurred at a time when intermarriage between Grenadians and Vincentian had been commonplace. As a consequence, a number of individuals on board the vanished schooner were originally from the island of St Vincent and included children from comparatively "well to do" families who were being educated in Grenada. Also travelling on the schooner *Island Queen* were several individuals from other neighbouring islands, including Trinidad and St Lucia.

Among the persons listed as lost were at least six separate groups of two or three siblings from well-known prominent families in St Vincent and Grenada. The numbers included two daughters of a well-respected Grenadian physician and his Vincentian wife. The sisters had been on their way to visit their maternal grandmother, who lived on the island of St Vincent. On board also were two daughters of an eminent Vincentian politician. They were pupils at the prestigious St Joseph Convent on the island of Grenada and were returning home for the holidays. The eminent Grenadian politician and editor of the island's main journal, T. A. Marryshow, lost a son and two daughters. It may have been the case that Mr Marryshow's positive and uplifting editorials during a period of uncertainty mirrored his personal fortitude in holding firmly and positively to the belief of an eventual happy outcome to an enigma that was yet to unfold.

There were in total a minimum of four separate sibling groups consisting of two or three members, but almost every "well-to-do" family in St George's town mourned the loss of at least one son or daughter. The children on board the schooner *Island Queen* were aged between 14 and 16 and had been pupils at St Joseph's Convent, Anglican High School or the Grenada Boys' Secondary School, commonly known as the GBSS.

The bright young adult passengers on the party schooner included teachers and civil servants, individuals who had recently completed higher education and were about to embark on promising careers; the beautiful young lady who had been applauded after being crowned Grenada's Carnival Queen of 1944; groups of best friends and work colleagues, boyfriend and girlfriend couples and one married couple. Several passengers had been invitees to a wedding that was arranged to take place on the Island of St Vincent on Monday, 7th August 1944, and relatives and specially invited guests of the owner and Captain of the ill-fated vessel were also among those presumed lost.

Ten members of the schooner's crew were included in the numbers lost. A child of the time who resided in a St George's suburb alleged that two close relatives had been working on the *Island Queen* when it disappeared. The particular crewmen were apparently covering for co-workers who were unable to work over the August Bank Holiday weekend due to previously arranged commitments.

The vast majority of the people who began a journey of pleasure to St Vincent on the schooner *Island Queen* on that historical day in August 1944 had been members of an exclusively elite section of the population. These confident and self-assured individuals were no doubt comfortable being in a party environment with people with whom they were able to identify. It was, as a consequence, of little surprise that every middle-class family who lived in the town of St George's lost either a father, mother, husband, wife, son, daughter, grandchild, uncle, aunt, niece, nephew, cousin or close friend on the vanished schooner; but, regardless of social divide, everyone in the town community knew everybody and was deeply affected by the catastrophic loss of lives.

Personal Accounts of How the Tragedy Impacted

Among the party people that were presumed to have been taken by the sea was the young man who arrived at the pier after the schooner *Island Queen* had departed from the harbour. In his eager determination to join the party and with ticket in hand, the individual hired a small fishing boat that quickly rowed him to the pleasure schooner. He was undoubtedly ecstatically relieved to have caught the boat "in the nick of time", but his relatives who shared his joy and wished him well were particularly bereft on hearing news of the Governor's conclusion regarding the unfortunate fate of the excursion vessel and all hands on board.

The enthusiastic reveller's nephew, a namesake of his uncle who went on to become a well-known and respected medical practitioner, was just four years of age when the schooner *Island Queen* set off on the highly anticipated journey of pleasure to the Island of St Vincent. The child of the age spoke of how the loss of a beloved son, brother, nephew, uncle and cousin impacted on the entire family.

The young party-goer had been one of two brothers to have perished during World War 2. The first brother, who joined the British Royal Air Force after volunteering to fight alongside Allied troops, was killed in action when his aircraft was brought down over Europe; and now one of only two surviving brothers was also gone. The zealousness applied by the young relative in ensuring his participation on the excursion was at the time reflected upon by family members. It was depressingly ironic to think that he had been hurrying to meet his fate. The mother of the deceased and maternal grandmother of our informant had been mentally and physically "crippled" to have lost two sons within such a short period of time. She took to her bed and was alleged to have grieved the loss of two precious offspring for many years thereafter.

A retired professional who was an 11-year-old schoolboy at the time of the *Island Queen* excursion, recounted how his father ignored his wife's advice against taking the trip and actually borrowed the funds required for securing his place on the pleasure excursion. But just days following the departure, the young boy was struck by a strong sense of foreboding, and "just knew" that his father would "never come back home".

The 11-year-old of the era and his younger siblings were not told by their mother or any other family member of Governor Grimble's presumed conclusion regarding the fate of the *Island Queen* and all hands on board, which included the beloved husband and father. It was a period in the community when children were shielded from matters considered inappropriate to be heard by their tender ears, but the siblings were sensitive to their mother's immense sadness and witnessed her emotional distress. They provided support by simply gathering around her and smothering her with affection. It was a situation that left no doubt in the mind of a young son that his initial intuition that his father would not be returning had been correct. He described his feelings at the time as being "gut-wrenching".

Many years passed before it was discovered that the distressed young widow had not fully grasped the fact that her husband and father of three young children had gone "for good". She was for an extended period convinced that he would one day be back in the family fold and spent many a long day, while the children were at school, peering through the window with a view of the harbour while wishing, praying and hoping that the missing schooner and passengers would appear.

A retired teacher, who was a pupil at St Joseph's Convent when the schooner *Island Queen* embarked on her journey of pleasure, reported that, among several teachers and students lost, were two of her very close school friends and the main teacher of her class. The woman revealed that, prior to receiving news regarding the presumed dreaded fate of the excursion vessel and all hands on board, everyone at the "Convent" truly believed that their missing friends and colleagues would one any day be back at school. Nonetheless, a regime of special prayers, which included

"The Rosary", had been put in place for their speedy return. These prayers were repeated at specific times each school day by every class and involved every nun, teacher and pupil. It was, as a consequence, a collectively unexpected and devastating "knock-back" when news of the presumed tragedy became known. In particular, young students had been deeply affected. Not only were they immensely shocked and saddened by the sudden and unexpected loss, but the tragedy brought into focus the children's own mortality at a stage when they may have felt themselves invincible. The catastrophe had been an unforgettable and difficult episode for students in every secondary school which had lost teachers and contemporaries. Children in elementary schools throughout the land were also sympathetically affected.

In similar action to other schools in the vicinity, children who attended the Convent were sent home for the rest of the day when conclusive news of the missing schooner broke in St George's. But subsequent to reopening on the following day, the Convent was filled with an atmosphere of gloom and doom. Nuns, teachers and pupils appeared dazed and depressed, and there were frequent emotional outbursts. Despite the prevailing sombreness, the school had been a source of support, comfort and solace. Everyone felt enabled to grieve and prayers were routinely offered for the souls of colleagues, pupils, friends and all those taken by the sea.

In spite of the overall climate of empathy within the community, only those who shared the catastrophic loss of loved ones could truly understand the consequential psychological trauma that persisted and which in some cases resulted in debilitating physical symptoms. There were those who developed heart conditions, suffered extreme high blood pressure and a few were felled by strokes. But the mental anguish was pronounced and unrelenting. The majority went off their food and became lethargic and lacked concentration. Deep depression, a lack of will to carry on, nightmares and sleeplessness were also experienced. Others, "paralysed" by emotional pain, became bed-bound.

The fact that the schooner *Island Queen* was lost at sea with no recovery of bodies and as a consequence being denied the opportunity of organising a funeral and by so doing achieve a measure of closure, must have been excruciatingly agonising for the immediate family of loved ones presumed to have perished at sea.

But there were a number of relatives and close friends who were unable to accept Governor Grimble's summarising conclusion that the schooner *Island Queen* must be presumed lost with "all hands on board". These particular relatives and close friends made it their duty to stand at the pier each day and await the arrival of their loved ones. Every new day came with renewed feelings of hope. They remained stoic in their conviction that the missing schooner and passengers would one day make a triumphant return.

Almost every relative of a loved one presumed lost may have been haunted by "if only" or "I wish" scenarios, and may have included: "I wish the excursion had never been organised", "I wish I hadn't given permission for my child or children to travel on the lost vessel", "I wish my loved one or close friend did not swap tickets", "If only my husband had listened to me when I suggested he should not go on the excursion", "If only my son, brother or uncle accepted the fact that he had missed the boat instead of paying to be hurriedly rowed to the cruising schooner", and "If only my father, son or brother did not leap from the *Providence Mark* and onto the *Island Queen* as the pleasure schooner was manoeuvring her way out of the harbour".

The schooner *Island Queen* disappeared during a period on the island of Grenada when professional counselling or therapy had been mainly unavailable or even unheard of. People relied on relatives and close friends for support during times of crisis. Solace and spiritual comfort were derived from prayer. But the broken families would never again become whole.

They Stepped Back from the Brink

One wonders whether it was by divine order or just coincidence that a number of intended party-goers teetered but for different unforeseen reasons stepped back from the brink at the very last minute. The persons that stepped back from the edge at the most timely of moments included a number of *Island Queen* ticket-holders who agreed to swap places with various unhappy excursionist who carried tickets for the schooner *Providence Mark*. The disgruntled excursionists had staged a "stand-in" on the party schooner *Island Queen*, on which they were determined to make the journey. The compromisers had been keen to bring to an end the seemingly intransigent situation. They were also anxious to begin the long-anticipated holiday excursion to the Island of St Vincent.

A 19-year-old young woman of the period, who resided with fairly "well-off" relatives in St George's town, recalled a wealthy entrepreneur who lived locally. He was allegedly the "one and only" millionaire on the island at the time. The successful Grenadian-born businessman was said to have visited the family home after the presumed fate of the *Island Queen* schooner and all hands on board had been officially declared. The visitor alleged that he had received a personal invitation from his friend, the Captain of the *Island Queen*. He was apparently very much looking forward to the trip, but changed his mind at the last minute. Apart from being unhappy about the later-than-scheduled start of the excursion, he was, for reasons unknown, unable to shift the disturbing thoughts of "funerals" that filled his head on the afternoon of 5th August.

There were allegedly several parents of "would-be" *Island Queen* revellers who, for a variety of last-minute concerns, withdrew their permission. A 19-year-old of the era spoke of an 18-year-old friend and member of the "elite club" whose father had wholeheartedly given his blessings to his daughter's participation on the pleasure excursion in company with close friends, and even purchased her ticket for the trip. On the morning of the excursion, the father of the young girl awoke with a disturbed expression and declared that he had "a bad dream" during the night which signalled potential risk to the safety and welfare of his child and promptly withdrew his consent to the trip. The young girl was hugely disappointed, but tearful pleadings held no sway with the parent, who was convinced that he had acted in his daughter's best interests.

There was also the known prospective party-goer who was suddenly taken ill with severe unexplained stomach pains and vomiting on the day of the excursion. The young man had been so unwell that he felt he had no choice but to cancel the trip at the very last moment.

A retired professional practitioner, who was a teenage pupil at St Joseph's Convent during the period, said that the man she went on to marry had purchased a ticket for the *Island Queen*. He was apparently very much looking forward to a journey of fun with his peers, but decided against going ahead with the planned trip after being plagued by a "bad feeling" on the day.

An informant, who at the time was a young resident in St George's town, told of a newly married couple who had secured tickets for the excursion, intending it to be a short honeymoon break. But the newly-weds became alarmed and decided to cancel the trip when the young wife was unexpectedly struck by continuous feelings of nausea. It was anticipated that her condition would be worsened by the sea journey and the tickets were regretfully passed on. The couple would later discover that the wife's sickness which determined the decision to cancel the proposed holiday break had been symptoms of early pregnancy. Their lives had been inadvertently saved by their unborn child and they thanked God for a very "luck escape".

Individuals who should have been on the excursion included various invited relatives and friends of the Captain of the pleasure schooner. These persons were, for various reasons, which may have included pre-arranged holiday commitments, unable to accept their personal invitation.

The escapees also included members of the regular crew who would normally have served on the schooner *Island Queen* at the time of the excursion. These crewmen may have chosen to be closer to home in company with relatives and friends over the fateful Bank Holiday weekend in August 1944.

Sensationalised truth-based or imagined accounts of people who should have been on the pleasure excursion but withdrew at the last moment were rumoured within the town community. Named persons were alleged to have been unable "to go" because they had been crucially required to cover for work colleagues. Others had apparently been struck by sudden illness or warned in a dream against taking the trip. It was also rumoured that several individuals had been so frustrated by the extended delayed departure that they had abandoned all notions of taking the planned trip, passed on their tickets to grateful holiday-makers and returned home.

Individuals who did not travel on the schooner *Island Queen* as previously planned would undoubtedly have experienced mixed emotions, including a deep sense of relief tinged with disturbing feelings of guilt. Moments of reflection and personal deliberations into probabilities of why they had been spared may have been a hauntingly recurring feature in their future lives. Was the scenario of the delayed departure that led to various individuals' decision to give up their places on the schooner *Island Queen* pre-ordained? Why did only certain individuals receive some form of premonition? Were they spared for a specific reason, or was it just not their time? Many believed that they had been protected by their "Guardian Angel". The mystery of life will remain unsolved. The "lucky escapees" and their relatives and friends would forever give thanks to the Almighty.

Action Taken by the Government of Grenada

Following the official closure, compensation payments were made to the next of kin of all Government employees. The amount paid had been bassed on the number of surviving dependants.

The search missions and surveillance that had been undertaken for locating, rescuing or recovering the missing schooner *Island Queen* and all persons on board were financed by appropriate authorities in Grenada and also St Vincent.

An Official Enquiry into the disappearance of the schooner *Island Queen* recommended by Governor Grimble in his conclusive memorandum dated 24th August 1944 was acted upon.

An Enquiry Commission was set up by the Grenada Government and the appointed Commissioners sat between 25th and 30th October 1944.

The findings of the Official Enquiry were laid out in a document placed before the Legislative Council on 8th December 1944.

Paragraph 1 of the document provided introductory basic information relating to the reasons for which the enquiry had been commissioned, and subsequently read as follows:

2. We sat between the 25th day of October and the 30th day of October, and heard the testimony of witnesses relating to matters which might assist us in determining the cause of the disappearance of the "Island Queen". We further heard testimony concerning the control exercised by the Port Authority of St George's, Grenada, over schooners clearing from that port, and examined the various Ordinances and Regulations of the Colony relating to shipping, particularly with regard to those touching the carrying of passengers. In this we conceive the terms of our Commission give us discretion to enquire not only into the loss of the "Island Queen" but also to explore any means which might lessen the risk of such a disaster occurring in the future and to make recommendations. This we have done.

3. In the course of our enquiry it was noticeable that there was considerable reluctance on the part of persons to come forward and assist us with our investigations. This reluctance did not extend outside the official proceedings

where rumours, often of an injurious and fantastic nature, were wildly believed. It is one of the purposes of this report to put an end to ill-informed statement.

4. In order for us to assess correctly certain points of evidence given before us and the probabilities arising therefrom, we found it necessary to hear expert opinion concerning the behaviour of schooners at sea and related matters of a technical nature. For this purpose we called Mr Sydney Lawrence Wells, who by reason of his experience as a schooner Master and his standing in the Colony seemed to us a suitable person.

5. No formal evidence has been heard on any matter relating to enemy action or to matters concerning our own Armed Forces by reason of the exigencies of war and the requirements of security. Where such matters are referred to in this report they are facts within the knowledge of the Commissioners themselves resting on information from the appropriate Naval Authority of the area.

It was further stated that the report had been "divided into six parts".

Part 1 consisted of a "narrative of events" and began with the date and time the *Island Queen* schooner departed from St George's, Grenada, bound for St Vincent; the number of passengers and crew; the date and time the schooner was expected to arrive at Kingstown harbour, St Vincent; and the date and time the *Island Queen* was reported missing.

Separately dated accounts of extensive air and sea search endeavours followed.

Part 2 contained a review of the measures taken when the *Island Queen* was reported overdue and stated:

> Taking into account the vagaries that must attend travel by sailing ship, anxiety over the non-arrival of the "Island Queen" at St Vincent was communicated to the responsible Authority at Grenada and also to the British Naval Authorities at Trinidad at an early stage. Subsequent search measures were undertaken promptly and no time was wasted. It becomes quite clear that responsible officials in Grenada did their utmost with the limited resources at their disposal.

> The wide sea areas involved necessitated the search being made principally from the air while surface vessels, apart from examining certain coastlines, were kept at immediate notice to follow up any reports received from aircraft. The search area was confined to the West of the Island Chain as the known winds and currents made it impossible for a disabled or drifting vessel to be found to the East The exact direction and speed of the wind and currents have not been closely investigated by the Commission as the scale of the search was such as to allow for every possible variation of speed and direction Northwest, West or Southwest.

> Although all participated, the principal burden of the search for the "Island Queen" fell upon the Aircraft of

the United States Navy. These Aircraft flew through fair weather and foul. The United States Naval Authorities employed large forces and continued their search far beyond the point where it might reasonably be assumed that further search would be fruitless. In all, a sea area of the order of two hundred thousand square miles was covered before the air search for the "Island Queen" was finally abandoned.

In spite of the vast and thorough search conducted, not a single piece of wreckage or other evidence of the "Island Queen" was found. This fact requires to be borne in mind when examining possible causes which might account for the disappearance of the vessel, and which are dealt with in Part III of the report.

We, the commissioners, are satisfied on the evidence before us that nothing was left undone which could possibly have been done in the institution and conduct of search measures after the "Island Queen" was reported overdue.

Under the heading "Investigation into the possible cause of the disappearance of the *Island Queen*", the report stated:

In view of the paucity of facts and the speculative nature of the problems involved in determining how the "Island Queen" came to disappear, we, the Commissioners, decided to explore the evidence in relation to the six possible ways in which a schooner in the circumstances of the "Island Queen" could reasonably be lost without trace, thereby hoping by elimination to narrow the field of investigation and arrive at a conclusion. We have therefore examined the relevant factors and probabilities under the headings which follow, giving our conclusions in each case.

(a) LOSS BY DIRECT ENEMY ACTION

It is within our knowledge that the area concerned was clear of the enemy at the relevant period, and we are satisfied that loss could not have been caused by direct enemy action either by submarine or any other force at the enemy's disposal.

(b) LOSS BY COLLISION AT SEA

There is no evidence to support such an assumption. A collision involves a second vessel and no report has been received from such a vessel, neither has any report of survivors or wreckage been received as should be expected in such circumstances. We are accordingly satisfied that loss was not occasioned by collision.

(c) LOSS BY STRANDING

There is no evidence to support a supposition of loss by stranding. There are no rocks or shoals in the waters through which the "Island Queen" was proceeding, neither has any wreckage been found on the coasts of the adjacent Islands as would be expected had the ship struck any of these. We therefore conclude that no loss by stranding took place.

(d) LOSS BY INTERNAL OR EXTERNAL EXPLOSION

Although a possibility exists that the "Island Queen" may have struck a floating mine, this possibility is very remote. Furthermore, it is unlikely that a floating mine met in this area would explode even if it were struck. We do not feel justified in accepting a most improbable solution in the absence of any evidence whatsoever to support it.

So far as an internal explosion is concerned, we are satisfied that any gasoline which may have been carried was small in quantity and stowed in a safe position away from engine and passengers, and that there is no reason to attribute loss from this cause.

(e) LOSS BY FIRE

There is no doubt that a conflagration sufficiently fierce to destroy utterly a ship of the size and construction of the "Island Queen" would be visible at a considerable distance. An expert witness is of the opinion that the glare from such a fire might be visible up to 15 miles at night and we, ourselves, are of the opinion that the smoke from such a fire in calm weather by day could be seen by an observer on the deck of a schooner up to a distance of 10 miles in good visibility. Statements of a witness support the view that so long as the "Island Queen" continued on her voyage under motor power any fire of the nature described would have been visible from the "Providence Mark". On the other hand, if the motor of the "Island Queen" had broken down no reliance can be placed on the fire on the "Island Queen" being seen from the "Providence Mark" after about 2 a.m. on the morning of 6th August. Even so, the course taken by the schooners suggests that fire of this kind would have been visible from the shore of the adjacent Islands. It is clearly established that no fire was seen from the "Providence Mark" and no report appears to have been received of a fire being observed from shore at the material time. (In this connection we desire to draw attention to unsubstantiated rumours emanating from the Island of Carriacou and Union Island that a blaze was seen at sea. No person has come forward to give evidence to support these rumours, which in themselves conflict in essential details, particularly in the matter of date, and which appear to be completely devoid of foundation.) The absence of any wreckage or other evidence of the "Island Queen" should also be taken into account in assessing the evidence of a fire at sea. It is established that the "Island Queen" was of stout construction, and it appears reasonable to assume that a fire, even though out of control, would take hold slowly. In these circumstances there seems to be no reason why boats could not have been got away which would subsequently have been found. Although loss by fire cannot be excluded, taking the evidence as a whole, we consider this to be unlikely and are disposed to look for the cause of loss elsewhere.

(f) LOSS BY FOUNDERING

A ship may founder by reason of capsizing, springing a leak, or being overwhelmed by heavy seas, or any combination of these. For the purpose of this enquiry, we can eliminate foundering through springing a leak or by reason of heavy seas. There is abundant evidence to show that the hull of "Island Queen" was sound and that a defect which had on a former occasion led to a leak through the stern gland had since been made good. Also there is satisfactory evidence that the weather in the area at the material time was generally good. There therefore remains the single question whether the disappearance of the "Island Queen" could have been due to foundering through capsizing. We have the support of expert opinion in stating that if the vessel had been struck on the beam by a sudden squall before the Master had time to shorten sail, then the ship would very probably capsize. The danger would be aggravated if at the time the vessel was almost stopped and if a substantial number of the passengers were upon the upper deck. No direct evidence is available, but we are in a position to examine certain related facts which have a bearing on the premises. Firstly, is a heavy squall likely in view of the weather experienced by the "Providence Mark"? The answer undoubtedly is yes, as squalls constantly abound in this area during the wet season, even though the weather is generally fine, while expert opinion has informed us that ships as close as five miles apart can experience different weather. Secondly, could the ship have been stopped or only been moving slowly? Evidence suggests a possibility that the engine of the "Island Queen" did break down about 8 p.m. on the 5th of August when her speed was noticed to have dropped as low as 4 knots. It is also legitimate in this connection to take into account the fact that the two Schooners seemed to be engaged in a race to see which one would reach St Vincent first and to remember that the "Providence Mark" had the better performance of the two under sail. If in these circumstances the engine of the "Island Queen" had been run at any time faster than at half speed, a breakdown would very probably have occurred in view of the known state of the engine. Thirdly, could the master of the vessel have been taken unawares by a sudden squall? The answer to this must lie in the extent to which the Master was pre-occupied, and generally in his skill as a seaman. The former is a matter of pure speculation, although if the engine had broken down at night it is not impossible that he may have been working on it and not appreciated the approach of a squall in the darkness. So far as the latter is concerned, we have no evidence before us to assess the skill of the Master or his crew under sail. We are, however, of the opinion that the Master of the "Island Queen" regarded his engine as the principal means of motive power and the sails as a secondary means, thus reversing the normal practice for auxiliary schooners. We are strengthened in this opinion by the known fact that the installation of engine and propeller chosen by the Master himself was of a kind to cause a marked deterioration in the sailing qualities of his ship.

Fourthly, if a squall struck the "Island Queen" when unprepared, would the ship recover easily? It would appear not. All the evidence tends to show that this ship was heavy and sluggish under sail. Fifthly, if the ship was lost by capsizing, would this be consistent with the absence of any discoverable wreckage? In our opinion this is precisely what would be expected. There is no reason to think that the normal practice of keeping hatches open in fair weather was not observed by the "Island Queen", and if so any inrush of water due to the ship turning over would sink her almost immediately in view of the 15 tons of ballast in the ship and the massive engine assembly estimated to weigh 7½ tons.

Bearing in mind all the circumstances and eliminating the other alternative causes of loss, none of which can be substantiated, we are inevitably led to the conclusion that loss by foundering through capsizing is not only a possibility but a probability.

Part IV of the document related to "Investigation into the Administration and control of the Schooner, particularly in relation to the safety of Passengers".

It became apparent during the course of the investigation that the "Shipping Rules" that were in place for governing the control of schooners "plying" from the port of St George, Grenada, were not being fully enforced, and that the rules themselves were in need of revision, particularly where they concerned the carriage of passengers. "It is observed that the Shipping Rules have not been reviewed since 1908!"

The Commission's Recommendations for the better safety of passengers travelling by sea from the Colony of Grenada were listed in Part V of the Report.

FINDINGS OF THE COMMISSION

> Although there is no direct evidence to determine the cause of the supposed loss of the Schooner "Island Queen", we are nevertheless of the opinion that this vessel might have foundered consequent on capsizing in a squall.

> We conclude that the Schooner "Island Queen" must be presumed lost by Marine hazard.

The signed document was dated 30th October 1944.

RESPONSES TO THE OFFICIAL ENQUIRY

The publication of the Commissioners' Official Enquiry into the supposed loss of the schooner *Island Queen* had been very much anticipated, not only by relatives and friends of those presumed lost, but also the people at large. In the absence of physical evidence, it was generally expected that every theoretical probability would have been put before the Board, and that each presented theory would in turn be fully and constructively debated, assessed, summarised and concluded.

But even before arriving at the body of the document, relatives and friends of the presumed deceased and everyone who initially accessed the publicised document were struck an unexpected blow on reading paragraph 5 of the introduction:

> No formal evidence has been heard on any matter relating to enemy action or to matters concerning our own Armed Forces by reason of the exigencies of war and the requirements of security.

Following the publication of Governor Grimble's conclusive memorandum regarding the fate of the schooner *Island Queen* and all hands on board and the termination of official search operations, various theories relating to the probable cause of the tragedy had been rumoured on the island of Grenada; and though the various rumoured theories were seen to have been fully addressed in the Enquiry document, the probability that was most believed by the nation had been omitted.

The majority of islanders suspected that the *Island Queen* had been torpedoed by Allied submarines on the night of 5th August and, on realising the mistake, every piece of evidence was scrupulously "cleared up" well before the schooner was reported missing.

The decision to exclude from the enquiry what had been generally deemed a most credible theory seemed a blatant "cover up" and the Enquiry was dismissed as nothing but a "whitewash". The people of Grenada harboured suspicions that their Government was withholding information about the tragedy and were, as a consequence, angry and outraged. The fact that the probability of friendly action was not considered because of the "requirements of security" meant nothing. As far as Grenadians were concerned, "establishing the truth" should have been the Commissioners' primary consideration. This was not proved to be the case and the Official Enquiry was judged to have fallen short of expectation and consequently lacked credibility.

Most importantly, the relatives and close friends of loved ones presumed to have been lost at sea were deeply disappointed and agonisingly distressed on reading the Enquiry Report. They very much hoped that the findings of the Enquiry would provide an element of peace that would enable the beginning of the process of coming to terms with the tragic and untimely loss of precious souls, and felt strongly that they had been cheated by a narrow, insensitive Enquiry. The memory of loved ones had been disrespected by the Commissioners' failure to conduct a fair and full investigation into all the probable causes for the catastrophe. The much-anticipated Enquiry had been an insult to the intelligence of relatives and close friends and served only to compound bitter feelings of loss.

The Commissioners' investigation into the administration and control of schooners, particularly relating to the safety of passengers, detailed in Part IV of the document, had, on the other hand, been generally well received.

It had been discovered during the Enquiry that "Shipping rules governing the control of schooners plying from the Port of St George, Grenada, were not being fully enforced and that the Rules themselves were in need of revision, particularly where they concerned the carriage of passengers. It is observed that the "Shipping Rules" have not been reviewed since the year 1908."

The five-point recommendations "for the better safety of passengers travelling by sea from the Colony of Grenada", were listed in paragraph V of the Report.

The Aftermath of the Official Enquiry on the Island of Grenada

When it was announced that a full Official Enquiry would be carried out for establishing the most likely cause for the loss of the schooner *Island Queen* and all hands on board, the existing climate of gloom that hung over the island lifted somewhat. Everyone, and in particular the relatives and close friends of loved ones presumed lost, expected that a broad-based objective exercise, inclusive of all probabilities, would be fully analysed before arriving at a reasoned determination in each case. But, consequent to the omission of the most-believed rumoured probability that the tragedy could have been the result of Allied action, the mood of the nation changed. The melancholy that had been temporarily replaced by cautious optimism during the course of the Enquiry was taken over by a climate of resentment. The community in the town of St George's was for an extended period of time engulfed in a vacuum of simmering fury, with passionate discussions and debates relating to the perceived injustice of the "rubbish" Enquiry being commonplace. Those who all along suspected that the Government had been withholding information were strongly of the view that they had been proven "right". It may have appeared that their Government had absolutely no clout and could do nothing but surrender to the Colonial powers all principles associated with self-determination and justice for the beloved departed. Moreover, any possible financial remuneration to bereaved families from Allied authorities shown to be accountable now appeared remote.

Apart from the emotional consequences, the sudden and unexpected losses also presented a life-changing financial crisis to families whose main breadwinner was no longer there and may have been a husband, father, wife or mother. And, though the next of kin and dependants of Government employees such as civil servants and teachers, presumed to have been lost on the *Island Queen* schooner, received compensation payments, the remuneration granted had been inadequate for the long-term financial needs of surviving family members. In particular, wives who had been previously comfortably supported by committed and responsible husbands found that they were, all of a sudden, having "to carry the can". Many were "strapped for cash", and various ways and means were contrived for bringing in much-needed pounds, shillings and pence to ensure the continued welfare of their offspring. There were those who also received assistance from members of their extended family networks and several bereaved families accepted invitations to move in and share the homes of more prosperous relatives.

A young boy of the era disclosed that his mother fell back on her skills as a "seamstress" and spent much of her day sitting at the sewing machine stitching outfits for customers. Children from country areas who attended secondary schools in the town of St George's were also taken in as paid boarders. The family would eventually move to America after they were sponsored by an "uncle" who lived and worked in the state of New York.

Although the bereaved struggled under the heavy burden of grief and pain, there remained a consistent flow of assistance, including practical, prayerful and emotional. A child of the day said that, on sensing their mother's distress, he would join with his two younger siblings in encircling and embracing the young widow. Indeed, they always remained close to their mother and the family were comforted by each other.

Time dragged on, hours turned into days, days became weeks, weeks evolved into months, Christmas and the New Year came and went. But the normally jovially celebrated festivities lacked lustre during the holiday period in 1944 and 1945. The people in the town of St George's had still not come to terms with the devastatingly unexpected fate of the *Island Queen* schooner with all hands on board and a collective sense of depression prevailed. It may not have felt "right" to be involved in street celebrations at a time when relatives and friends of the presumed deceased, and the community at large, mourned the sad losses.

World War 2 Ends

Grenadians became aware that World War 2 had ended with victory for the Allies. The most welcome of news was announced by the then British Prime Minister, Sir Winston Churchill, on BBC overseas radio on the morning of 8th May 1945.

The triumphant breaking news was quickly spread across the island of Grenada and, as in many countries around the world, gave rise to national celebrations. After several years of austerity, the St George's folk, along with others up and down the island, felt compelled to cast aside their troubles for a while and embrace wholeheartedly the announced victory.

The exhilarated majority spilled noisily onto the streets in droves and demonstrated their delight and extreme sense of relief. They waved flags, blew whistles and shells, beat on steel drums, danced energetically and sang loudly to a backdrop of chiming church bells. A town resident of the day, who participated in the jollifications, said: "We really enjoyed ourselves. It was even better than Carnival!"

When it was announced that a victory parade had been planned and would be taking place in the island's city the following day, a large number of people from around congregated in the market place on the morning of 9th May 1945. They waited patiently and expectantly under the heat of the sun for the ceremony to begin, and were not disappointed when eventually the events were presented. The island's Governor, dignitaries and politicians were in attendance as police officers, soldiers from the Southern Defence Force, the Volunteer Reserve, cadets, Boy Scouts and Girl Guides saluted and marched proudly in unison to military tunes played by the city's police band. It had indeed been a fulfilling and unforgettable moment of national pride.

The return of fathers, sons, husbands and sweethearts who had volunteered to serve alongside Allied forces had been a joyous relief for their respective family members and close friends. These courageous young men were welcomed home as heroes. Many were rewarded by being offered work posts in the Civil Service. Professional workers such as teachers were reinstated. Individuals who had been employed in the private sector prior to going to war were able to resume positions that had been left open pending their return.

In time, import and export trading would again be productive and commodities become increasingly accessible. Even so, a schoolboy of the period clearly recalled his family having to use their ration book for purchasing essential items for a considerable period after war was declared over. But restrictions on gasoline that had been put in place were lifted and reflected by the increased number of vehicles on the road.

Although the end of World War 2 came with a return to normality and a promise of better times ahead, the community in the town of St George's and, in particular, relatives and close friends of lost souls on the schooner *Island Queen*, remained haunted by the tragedy.

Time Heals?

Time moved on, but for many whose loved ones were presumed to have "gone down" with the schooner *Island Queen* on the unprecedented pleasure excursion, time was at a standstill. Not knowing "for sure" what happened to their loved ones and in particular not having a body to lay to rest or being able to say goodbye, meant that there was no closure for grieving relatives.

There were those who remained in denial long after the *Island Queen* vanished. These individuals were convinced that their beloved family member or close friend would one day return. And several forever hopefuls maintained a vigil at the Island's pier. A schoolboy of the day spoke of his mother being glued to a window at the family home which overlooked the town's harbour. The young widow had been among many unable to "let go" the belief that loved ones would without doubt "come back home". After all, no one knew what was in store on every new day and for some hope was never dimmed.

Moving on had been particularly difficult for the parents of the presumed deceased. Many gave up the will to carry on and for some enduring psychological trauma severely impacted on their physical health and well-being. A number of these traumatised family members were reported to have developed serious life-threatening conditions such as cardio or elevated hypertension. The report in the *Vincentian* newspaper – even before the presumed tragic loss was officially declared – that the father of two sisters missing on the schooner *Island Queen* had been hospitalised, offered credence to the allegations. The eminent gentleman had collapsed with high blood pressure. There could be no doubting this father's condition had been triggered by uncertainty and heightened anxiety regarding the vanished vessel and all on board. Several family members would eventually succumb to illnesses that were brought on by their tragic loss.

As the years passed, the agonising heartache felt by relatives and friends may have dulled somewhat as they learnt to live with their lamentable sense of loss. But they had been "haunted" by the tragedy and beneath psychological scars lay wounds that remained unhealed. Grieving families never truly recovered from the shocking and untimely demise of loved ones. Despite being surrounded by empathetic support, professional assistance with overcoming their grief may not have been available during the period.

These assumptions are supported by comments made by several surviving relatives and friends of those who were presumed to have perished at sea and included:

"You know, my grandmother never got over it."

"Still can't believe that my beautiful and vivacious friend never came back to school."

"It always felt like someone was missing from the group. The gap was never filled."

"Still can't believe what happened."

"You know, I still think about her every day."

And with reference to a much-loved father, "I missed the old man dreadfully and still do."

The emotions displayed when the requested comments were delivered revealed that, below healed surfaces, lay emotional and psychological wounds that were as raw as the day loved ones were declared lost at sea.

The unprecedented circumstances surrounding the ill-fated *Island Queen* schooner remained an enigma among the people of Grenada and in particular the community of St George's, where the majority of revellers on the pleasure schooner lived. Every individual in the small city of the period knew each other and the tragedy was for many years recounted in tones that echoed undimmed shock and awe.

The circumstances surrounding the unprecedented pleasure excursion, and the shockingly tragic outcome that shook the island to its very core, was passed from generation to generation.

Hypotheses

It was apparent that those questioned harboured grievance and suspicions regarding the Official Enquiry, which they still believe was a complete "whitewash".

Most remained steadfast in the belief that the schooner *Island Queen* had been destroyed by the Allied Naval forces when it was detected by sonar that the vessel carried a German engine; and on discovering their mistake, all the evidence, including debris and floating bodies, was hurriedly "cleared up" well before the schooner was reported missing. It was a theory that had not been investigated by the Commissioners of the Official Enquiry undertaken in Grenada between 25th and 30th October 1944.

An individual questioned expressed the personal view that Allied ships became alarmed on hearing noises from the

Island Queen. They may have anticipated danger and in an action of self-defence slammed into and torpedoed the pleasure schooner.

Another held the opinion that the *Island Queen* schooner lost buoyancy as it cruised over "Kick 'em Jenny" and sank. Kick 'em Jenny is an area of the Caribbean Sea between Grenada and Carriacou, under which lies an active volcano. Ships had always been known to experience turbulence when sailing in the location.

A gentleman echoed the voice of the majority when he said that the lost schooner had been sunk by an Allied submarine as a result of having a German engine.

A totally different but strongly held conviction was that the schooner had not been sunk. The vessel was captured and taken to a faraway land where the Captain, passengers and crew were abandoned to their own devices.

It was reported by various persons on the sister excursion schooner *Providence Mark* that the *Island Queen* was last spotted on the horizon at around midnight on 5th August 1944 and was alleged to have been travelling at speed. If that was the case, she would have already passed the danger area known as Kick 'em Jenny.

The schooner's German engine may have been detected by sonar equipment and as a consequence been taken down by an Allied submarine. But was the subsequent suspected "clean-up" operation so scrupulous that absolutely no evidential clues were spotted during repeated air and sea searches? And how were the bodies disposed of?

The *Island Queen* could have simply lost buoyancy and sunk. If that was the case, it could not have occurred over Kick 'em Jenny, as suggested. The Captain of the parallel excursion schooner, *Providence Mark*, reported that the *Island Queen* was last seen after dusk, at the sea's horizon and travelling very fast.

It is possible that the schooner may have been struck and sunk by a rogue wave. Rogue waves are extreme storm waves of approximately 20 metres or more (in excess of 60 feet). Rogue waves, also known as freak or killer waves, are very unpredictable, come unexpectedly and can appear in completely calm seas.

There is also the possibility that that the *Island Queen* was sunk by friendly fire. The schooner had been alleged to have been sailing far out at sea as she headed for the island of St Vincent. It was during a period when battles in Caribbean waters were not uncommon.

The Commissioners of the Official Enquiry concluded that the schooner *Island Queen* might have foundered consequent to capsizing in a squall and must be presumed lost by Marine hazard. On the contrary, the Captain of the schooner *Providence Mark* alleged that the weather was fine on the night of the excursion and there were, "no squalls or anything to worry about".

A Mystery of the Sea

What actually happened that resulted in the loss of the schooner *Island Queen* during her pleasure journey to the island of St Vincent on the night of Saturday/Sunday, 5th/6th August 1944 will forever be a mystery, but may remain a topic of objective or subjective speculation or opinion.

Although surveillance and air and sea searches had been conducted in repeated endeavours to locate, rescue or recover the missing schooner and/or missing individuals, no underwater missions had been undertaken. A ship could not simply vanish into thin air while sailing on open waters and it is generally accepted that the schooner *Island Queen*, for reasons unknown, sank during her voyage from Grenada to the neighbouring island of St Vincent. Consequently, oblivion would most likely have been instantaneous and at a joyous moment; and revellers with happy faces are resting peacefully within the wreck of the schooner that is embedded at the bottom of the ocean.

Emotional, psychological and even physical pain would have been endured only by loved ones left behind.